D0438867

DATE DUE

JUN 8 2005			
GAYLORD			PRINTED IN U.S.A.

The
Dachshund

An Owner's Guide To

A HAPPY HEALTHY PET

JACKSON COUNTY LIBRARY SERVICES
MEDFORD, OREGON 97501

Howell Book House
A Simon & Schuster Macmillan Company
1633 Broadway
New York, NY 10019

Copyright © 1995 by **Howell Book House**
All rights reserved. No part of this book may be reproduced or transmitted in any form or by any means, electronic or mechanical, including photocopying, recording, or by any information storage and retrieval system, without permission in writing from the Publisher.

MACMILLAN is a registered trademark of Macmillan, Inc.

Library of Congress Cataloging-in-Publication Data
Carey, Anne (Anne Carol)
The dachshund: an owner's guide to a happy, healthy pet
p. cm.
Includes bibliographical references.

ISBN: 0-87605-386-X

1. Dachshunds. I. Title.
SF429.D35C37 1995
636.7'53—dc20   95-15662
            CIP

Manufactured in the United States of America
10 9 8 7 6 5 4 3 2 1

Series Director: Dominique De Vito
Series Assistant Director: Felice Primeau
Book Design: Michele Laseau
Cover Design: Iris Jeromnimon
Illustration: Jeff Yesh
Photography:
  Cover Photos by Paulette Braun/Pets by Paulette
  Courtesy of the American Kennel Club: 20
  Joan Balzarini: 30, 96
  Mary Bloom: 29, 96, 136, 145
  Paulette Braun/Pets by Paulette: 2–3, 6, 8, 12, 38, 61, 70, 96
  Buckinghamhill American Cocker Spaniels: 148
  Ann Carey: 32, 51, 62, 91
  Sian Cox: 134
  Dr. Ian Dunbar: 98, 101, 103, 111, 116–117, 122, 123, 127
  Trudy Kawami: 24, 29, 40, 52
  Gina Leone: 36–37, 45, 58
  Dan Lyons: 5, 11, 16, 96
  Cathy Merrithew: 129
  Liz Palika: 133
  Janice Raines: 132
  Susan Rezy: 96-97
  Judith Strom: 22, 27, 33, 41, 43, 44, 47, 57, 64, 66, 68, 78, 96, 107, 110, 128, 130, 135, 137, 139, 140, 144, 149, 150
  Kerrin Winter & Dale Churchill: 56
Production Team: Troy Barnes, John Carroll, Jama Carter, Kathleen Caulfield, Trudy Coler, Vic Peterson, Terri Sheehan, Marvin Van Tiem, Amy DeAngelis and Kathy Iwasaki

Contents

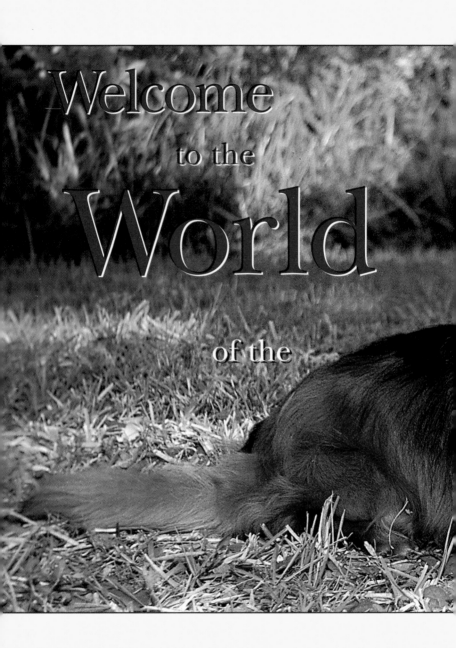

Welcome
to the
World
of the

part one

Dachshund

External Features of the Dachshund

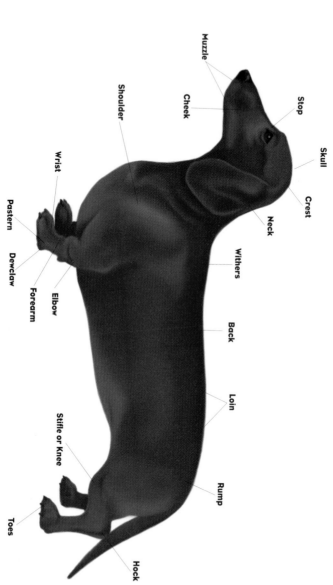

chapter 1

What
is a
Dachshund?

The Dachshund, like most breeds, has a loyal following in all parts of the world. Those who are lucky enough to be owned by one usually can't venture far from their doorstep before someone approaches to extol the virtue of this lively, alert companion who reminds them of a dog from their youth, the one waiting for them at home or the one they recently lost.

Before one understands how the Dachshund thinks and responds to life around him, one must be aware of what the Dachshund is, how he is put together and what he was bred to do!

Sizes and Coat Types

One of the best things about the Dachshund is that he comes in two sizes—Standard and Miniature. While there is no absolute limit for the Standard, the Dachshund Club of America suggests that he range from sixteen to thirty-two pounds. The Miniature, on the other hand, is carefully monitored. At twelve months of age, he must be eleven pounds or under— and should remain so. Other than the weight classification, there is no difference between the two sizes. The purpose of the dog and the standard by which he is judged are the same.

These long-haired Dachshunds are one of three coat types in the breed.

In addition to the two sizes, the Dachshund also comes in three coat varieties—smooth (short hair), long- and wirehaired. The appearance of each variety is altered by coat type only. What makes each variety different is clearly discussed under the "coat" heading in the official breed standard, written by the Dachshund Club of America (referred to as the "parent club" of the breed) and approved by the American Kennel Club, which is the largest governing body of registered purebred dogs in this country. Unlike horses, the canine is not a thoroughbred but a purebred. The word itself says it plainly—a dog bred pure to his breed standard for at least five generations.

The Dachshund Club of America (DCA) was formed in 1895 and chose to adopt, with certain modifications, the 1879 standard set down by the German Teckel Klub, which was a combination of all preexisting Dachshund clubs in Germany at that time.

The first official standard of the DCA was written and approved by the AKC in July of 1935. Since that time, it has been amended twice; once in 1971 and then again in 1992. The latest version is the one included at the end of this chapter.

One of the reasons that the standard has been amended was to change the weight classification for the Miniatures. In 1935, the standard read "under nine pounds"; in 1971, it was amended to "under ten pounds"; in 1992, it was worded as "eleven pounds and under." All of these weights referred to the Miniature at twelve months or older.

What about Faults?

What makes a fault serious, minor, secondary? For example, Wall eyes (blue) except in the case of dapples are a *serious* fault since the standard calls for eyes to be "very dark in color."

Also, "teeth fit closely together in a scissors bite. An even bite is a *minor* fault. Any other deviation is a *serious* fault." "A small amount of white on the chest (smooth coat) is acceptable but *not* desirable"; "the eyes are almond shaped." Therefore, a round eye is acceptable but *not* preferred.

When do these things matter? In the show ring—particularly when a judge compares individual dogs to the standard in order to determine class placements—and when a breeder is evaluating a litter and compares individual puppies to the standard, not to one another, as potential show and breeding prospects.

There is much in all breed standards, however, that is subjective. For example, how long is a "long" ear? How far forward is "not too far"? How do you measure "not too broad nor too narrow"?

> ### WHAT IS A BREED STANDARD?
>
> A breed standard—a detailed description of an individual breed—is meant to portray the *ideal* specimen of that breed. This includes ideal structure, temperament, gait, type—all aspects of the dog. Because the standard describes an ideal specimen, it isn't based on any particular dog. It is a concept against which judges compare actual dogs and breeders strive to produce dogs. At a dog show, the dog that wins is the one that comes closest, in the judge's opinion, to the standard for its breed. Breed standards are written by the breed parent clubs, the national organizations formed to oversee the well-being of the breed. They are voted on and approved by the members of the parent clubs.

Many of the finer points may seem unimportant to you when, in fact, they are essential. If you study the standard as it is written, it defines the basic outline of the dog, the muscle tone, the overall appearance of the Dachshund as he should be (there is no perfect dog) and what you can expect your dog to do and not to do. And, as you read this standard, try to remember that the whole is greater than the parts. We need to see how the pieces meld together to make this little dog what he is.

The Important Details

The Dachshund is low to the ground but should not be

dragging the ground, and as the standard states, he should move with agility. He should be bold and confident in the carriage of his head and possess an "intelligent, alert facial expression." That statement is a perfect example of the subjectivity found in most breed standards. "Intelligent facial expression"? Not to worry. You will know that when you see it—eyes that grab you with their alert "I love the world" attitude, a head carried like "I own the world and you, I can tackle anything. Want to see?"

The Dachshund is a lively, alert companion.

Since temperament is uppermost, this is what the Dachshund is supposed to be: "clever, lively and courageous to the point of rashness." Word for word, "Any display of shyness is a *serious* fault." A puppy raised in the proper environment should come to you willingly, with tail wagging. She will also *not* come to you, with tail wagging, just as well! Her sense of comic fun will often lead you on a merry chase, and her agility and speed will amaze you! She is, as the standard says, "clever" and "agile"!

She also perseveres! She is agile enough to squeeze out of any door or gate you try to close behind you should she feel she wants to come along! She is people-oriented and she is an extrovert. (Chapter 3 will deal in more depth with his views on life.) She will outsmart and out-think you any time the chance arises. She does not, at any time, consider herself a small dog. Never take her for granted.

Many people poke fun at the short-legged, long little dog. However, it is important to remember that while one may never use the Dachshund to hunt, she *was bred* to hunt! She is powerful, muscular and athletic. In the field, she must "give tongue." This means exactly what it says—the Dachshund *barks!* (How to deal with this will be discussed in Chapter 3.)

He is a scent hunter, and when he hunts, he is single-minded. When he goes to ground, he is a formidable foe. His jaws and teeth are strong and powerful. Consider the purpose for which he was bred: to track, dig to his prey, corner it, and bark to alert the above-ground hunter exactly where in the myriad of dens the animals are. Then the hunter can either dig to the Dachshund or assist the dog in retreating from the earth if he does not emerge with his prey.

The Dachshund's nose, with the help of his length of ear, picks up the scent and he is off on her mission. If he did not "give tongue" as he worked, the hunters would be hard pressed to follow, as the Dachshund does not travel in a straight line when tracking and once gone to ground, locating him would indeed be a challenge if not for the melodious tonguing of a dog who has cornered his prey.

The ideal Dachshund must be well-balanced. And one of the most important aspects of the standard is the neck and forequarters. "A long neck, muscular and clean cut, flows gracefully into the shoulder." A short neck directly affects the shoulder placement and poor angulation in the neck does not allow the dog proper reach when moving forward.

In the hunting Dachshund we need stamina over speed. Short-legged hounds hunt with endurance. Therefore, the Dachshund hock must be strong: "From the rear, the thighs are strong and powerful. The metatarsus—short and strong and when viewed from behind they are upright and parallel."

If these aspects of the hunting hound are not as correct as they should be, it hampers the performance and the stamina and thus may cause injury to the dog in the field.

Since the body of the Dachshund is long, the dog must have "well-sprung ribs ample enough and oval enough to allow complete development of heart and lungs, with the keel merging gradually into the line of the abdomen and extending well beyond the front legs." This dog must have the capacity to breathe underground and the muscular agility that enables him to maneuver the earth when he goes to ground. He needs to be low enough to slide into the earth and yet have enough leg under him to prevent injury to himself. His hindquarters must be strong enough to propel him forward and to keep his keel and powerful forechest from scraping the ground. It is the balance of the forechest, brisket and hocks working together, along with the elasticity of his muscles, that enables this hound to move with ease through the maze of underground tunnels. He must be muscular, with no skin loose enough to allow his prey to grab hold, which is why the standard states that there should be no wrinkles or dewlap.

It is comparable to the knit clothing people wear; the skin of the Dachshund should fit close to the body and yet stretch to allow her to move and bend as necessary when she is working.

When the Dachshund moves, her gait should be "fluid and smooth." Her forelegs should "reach well forward without much lift." Simply put, she should not paddle the air or prance. Such movements are wasted energy for a dog bred for stamina.

Viewed from the front, the legs do not move in exact parallel planes but incline slightly inward. This has to happen due to the shortness of leg and the width of the chest. When the dog is viewed from the rear, "the thrust of correct movement is seen when the pads are clearly exposed. Short choppy movement, rolling, being too close or too wide coming or going are incorrect."

To keep the topline level in motion, each vertebra must be supported by ribs, tendons, pelvis and muscles. This means, simply, that the length of ribbing and topline balance one another.

The Dachshund must have agility, freedom of movement and endurance to do the work for which the breed was developed. As you read the breed standard, you will learn that the miniature carries bone and substance appropriate for her weight, and since the Dachshund is a dog of substance and stamina, both sizes should possess "robust muscular development." The words "strong," "powerful" and "muscular" appear quite often in the standard for a reason!

The Dachshund's neck should flow gracefully into the shoulder.

Once you become acquainted with the standard, you will appreciate the form and function of the Dachshund. The following pages will explain and clarify the development of this delightful hound and the way he views his world and the people in it!

The Official AKC Standard of The Dachshund

General Appearance Low to ground, long in body and short of leg with robust muscular development, the skin is elastic and pliable without excessive wrinkling. Appearing neither crippled, awkward, nor cramped in his capacity for movement, the Dachshund is well-balanced with bold and confident head carriage and intelligent, alert facial expression. His hunting spirit, good nose, loud tongue and distinctive build make him well-suited for below-ground work and for beating the bush. His keen nose gives him an advantage over most other breeds for trailing. NOTE: Inasmuch as the Dachshund is a hunting dog, scars from honorable wounds shall not be considered a fault.

Size, Proportion, Substance Bred and shown in two sizes, standard and miniature. Miniatures are not a separate classification but compete in a class division for "11 pounds and under at 12 months of age and older." Weight of the standard size is usually between 16 and 32 pounds.

Head Viewed from above or from the side, the head tapers uniformly to the tip of the nose. The eyes are of medium size, almond-shaped and dark-rimmed, with an energetic,

pleasant expression; not piercing; very dark in color. The bridge bones over the eyes are strongly prominent. Wall eyes, except in the case of dappled dogs, are a serious fault. The ears are set near the top of the head, not too far forward, of moderate length, rounded, not narrow, pointed, or folded. Their car-

Dachshunds are bold and confident.

riage, when animated, is with the forward edge just touching the cheek so that the ears frame the face. The skull is slightly arched, neither too broad nor too narrow, and slopes gradually with little perceptible stop into the finely-formed, slightly arched muzzle. Black is the preferred color of the nose. Lips are tightly stretched, well covering the lower jaw. Nostrils well open. Jaws opening wide and hinged well back of the eyes, with strongly developed bones and teeth. Teeth—Powerful canine teeth; teeth fit closely together in a scissors bite. An even bite is a minor fault. Any other deviation is a serious fault.

Neck Long, muscular, clean-cut, without dewlap, slightly arched in the nape, flowing gracefully into the shoulders.

Trunk The trunk is long fully muscled. When viewed in profile, the back lies in the straightest possible line between the withers and the short very slightly arched loin. A body that hangs loosely between the shoulders is a serious fault. Abdomen—Slightly drawn up.

Forequarters For effective underground work, the front must be strong, deep, long and cleanly muscled. Forequarters in detail: Chest—The breastbone is strongly prominent in front so that on either side a depression or dimple appears. When viewed from the front, the thorax appears oval and extends downward to the mid-point of the forearm. The enclosing structure of well-sprung ribs appears full and oval to allow, by its ample capacity, complete development of heart and lungs. The keel merges gradually into the line of the abdomen and extends well beyond the front legs. Viewed in profile, the lowest point of the breast line is covered by the front leg. Shoulder Blades—Long, broad, well-laid back and firmly placed upon the fully developed thorax, closely fitted at the withers, furnished with hard yet pliable muscles. Upper Arm—Ideally the same length as the shoulder blade and at right angles to the latter, strong of bone and hard of muscle, lying close to the ribs, with elbows close to the body, yet capable of free movement. Forearm—Short; suppled with hard yet pliable muscles on the front and outside, with tightly stretched tendons on the inside and at the back, slightly curved inwards. The joints between the forearms and the feet (wrists) are closer together than the shoulder joints, so that the front does not appear absolutely straight. Knuckling over is a disqualifying fault. Feet—Front paws are full, tight, compact, with well-arched toes and tough, thick pads. They may be equally inclined a trifle outward. There are five toes, four in use, close together with a pronounced arch and strong, short nails. Front dewclaws may be removed.

Hindquarters Strong and cleaned muscled. The pelvis, the thigh, the second thigh, and the metatarsus are ideally the same length and form a series of right angles. From the rear, the thighs are strong and powerful. The legs turn neither in nor out. Metatarsus—short and strong, perpendicular to the second thigh bone. When viewed from behind, they are upright and parallel. Feet—Hind Paws—Smaller than the front paws with four compactly closed and arched toes with tough, thick pads. The entire foot points straight ahead and is balanced equally on the ball and not merely on the toes. Rear dewclaws should be removed. Croup—Long, rounded and full, sinking slightly toward the tail. Tail—Set in continuation of the spine, extending without kinks, twists, or pronounced curvature, and not carried too gaily.

Gait Fluid and smooth. Forelegs reach well forward, without much lift, in unison with the driving action of the hind legs. The correct shoulder assembly and wellfitted elbows allow the long, free stride in front. Viewed from the front, the legs do not move in exact parallel planes, but incline slightly inward to compensate for shortness of leg and width of chest. Hind legs drive on a line with the forelegs, with hocks (metatarsus) turning neither in nor out. The propulsion of the hind leg depends on the dog's ability to carry the hind leg to complete extension. Viewed in profile, the forward reach of the hind leg equals the rear extension. The thrust of correct movement is seen when the rear pads are clearly exposed during rear extension. Feet must travel parallel to the line of motion with no tendency to swing out, cross over, or interfere with each other. Short, choppy movement, rolling or high-stepping gait, close or overly wide coming or going are incorrect. The Dachshund must have agility, freedom of movement, and endurance to do the work for which he was developed.

Temperament The Dachshund is clever, lively and courageous to the point of rashness, perservering in above and below ground work, with all the senses well-developed. Any display of shyness is a serious fault.

Special Characteristics of the Three Coat Varieties The Dachshund is bred with three varieties of coat: (1) smooth; (2) wirehaired; (3) longhaired and is shown in two sizes, standard and miniature. All three varieties and both sizes must conform to the characteristics already specified. The following features are applicable for each variety:

Smooth Dachshund Coat—Short, smooth and shining. Should be neither too long nor too thick. Ears not leathery. Tail—Gradually tapered to a point, well but not too richly haired. Long sleek bristles on the underside are considered a patch of strong-growing hair, not a fault. A brush tail is a fault, as is a partly or wholly hairless tail. Color of Hair— Although base color is immaterial, certain patterns and basic colors predominate. One-colored Dachshunds include red (with or without a shading of interspersed dark hairs or sable) and cream. A small amount of white on the chest is acceptable, but not desirable. Nose and nails—black.

Two-colored Dachshunds include black, chocolate, wild boar, gray (blue) and fawn (Isabella), each with tan markings over the eyes, on the sides of the jaw and underlip, on the inner edge of the ear, front legs, on the paws and around the anus, and from there to about one-third to one-half of the length of the tail on the underside. Undue prominence or extreme lightness of tan markings is undesirable. Nose and nails—in the case of black dogs, black; for chocolate and all other colors, dark brown, but self-colored is acceptable. Dappled Dachshunds—The "single" dapple pattern is expressed as lighter-colored areas contrasting with the darker base color, which may be any acceptable color. Neither the light nor the dark color should predominate. Nose and nails are the same as for one- and two-colored Dachshunds. Partial or wholly blue (wall) eyes are as acceptable as dark eyes. A large area of white on the chest of a dapple is permissible.

Brindle is a pattern (as opposed to a color) in which black or dark stripes occur over the entire body although in some specimens the pattern may be visible only in the tan points.

Wirehaired Dachshund Coat—With the exception of jaw, eyebrows, and ears, the whole body is covered with a uniform tight, short, thick, rough, hard outer coat but with finer, somewhat softer, shorter hairs (undercoat) everywhere distributed between the coarser hairs. The absence of an undercoat is a fault. The distinctive facial furnishings include a beard and eyebrows. On the ears the hair is shorter than on the body, almost smooth. The general arrangement of the hair is such that the wirehaired Dachshund, when viewed from a distance, resembles the smooth. Any sort of soft hair in the outercoat, wherever found on the body, especially on the top of the head, is a fault. The same is true of long, curly, or wavy

---

THE AMERICAN KENNEL CLUB

Familiarly referred to as "the AKC," the American Kennel Club is a nonprofit organization devoted to the advancement of purebred dogs. The AKC maintains a registry of recognized breeds and adopts and enforces rules for dog events including shows, obedience trials, field trials, hunting tests, lure coursing, herding, earthdog trials, agility and the Canine Good Citizen program. It is a club of clubs, established in 1884 and composed, today, of over 500 autonomous dog clubs throughout the United States. Each club is represented by a delegate; the delegates make up the legislative body of the AKC, voting on rules and electing directors. The American Kennel Club maintains the Stud Book, the record of every dog ever registered with the AKC, and publishes a variety of materials on purebred dogs, including a monthly magazine, books and numerous educational pamphlets. For more information, contact the AKC at the address listed in Chapter 13, "Resources," and look for the names of their publications in Chapter 12, "Recommended Reading."

hair, or hair that sticks out irregularly in all directions. Tail—Robust, thickly haired, gradually tapering to a point. A flag tail is a fault. Color of Hair—While the most common colors are wild boar, black and tan, and various shades of red, all colors are admissible. A small amount of white on the chest, although acceptable, is not desirable. Nose and nails—same as for the smooth variety.

Longhaired Dachshund Coat—The sleek, glistening, often slightly wavy hair is longer under the neck and on fore-

chest, the underside of the body, the ears, and behind the legs. The coat gives the dog an elegant appearance. Short hair on the ear is not desirable. Too profuse a coat which masks type, equally long hair over the whole body, a curly coat, or a pronounced parting on the back are faults. Tail—Carried gracefully in prolongation of the spine; the hair attains its greatest length here and forms a veritable flag. Color of Hair—Same as for the smooth Dachshund. Nose and nails same as for the smooth.

The foregoing description is that of the ideal Dachshund. Any deviation from the above described dog must be penalized to the extent of the deviation keeping in mind the importance of the contribution of the various features toward the basic original purpose of the breed.

DISQUALIFICATION Knuckling over of front legs.

Approved April 7, 1992

Effective May 27, 1992

chapter 2

The Dachshund's Ancestry

The early history of many of our purebred dogs is often woven through the legends and stories of several countries. The Dachshund is no exception. Some researchers think that a dog resembling this breed was pictured on Egyptian tombs, making the Dachshund more than 4,000 years old.

The Dachshund's Roots

This theory, along with others that place the dog in countries from Peru to the Orient, seems rather intangible, though "a book published in 1896 written by a Major Emil Ilgner claims that the Dachshund's history could be traced back through 35 centuries" (Lois Meistrell, *The New Dachshund*, Howell Book House: New York, 1989). It is commonly agreed that the Dachshund as we know him came out of

17

Germany. John Hutchinson Cook, known until his death in 1994 as "Mr. Dachshund" by those in the dog world, and a noted breeder and judge, had done endless research on this breed, which was so close to his heart. He felt that the Dachshund might have come to Germany when the Hapsburg heir, Maximilian, journeyed from Vienna to wed the daughter of the Duke of Burgundy in 1477. His future father-in-law, Charles the Bold, maintained hunting hounds by the thousands as well as extensive land holdings, since it is a well-known fact that in those times hunting and hunting hounds were pleasures afforded the wealthy nobles.

Some of these hounds, owned by Charles, the Duke of Burgundy, accompanied those who had journeyed with Maximilian when they returned home to Austria, where they were used to hunt in packs. Mr. Cook felt strongly that from those original Burgundy hounds, who were selectively bred down the centuries, the Dachshund evolved.

Whatever the theories one holds, the Dachshund as we know him today was developed and refined by the German foresters into what they needed—a fearless hunter with intelligence who could work above and below ground over various terrains, who was obstinate and rash enough to hold his prey at bay until the hunter could finish the deed. The prey ranged from rabbit and fox to badger and wild boars. This is where the Dachshund's piercing bark came in handy, enabling a pack of Dachshunds to corner but not necessarily kill. Usually, the hunter killed the quarry. One Dachshund

WHERE DID DOGS COME FROM?

It can be argued that dogs were right there at man's side from the beginning of time. As soon as human beings began to document their existence, the dog was among their drawings and inscriptions. Dogs were not just friends, they served a purpose: There were dogs to hunt birds, pull sleds, herd sheep, burrow after rats—even sit in laps! What your dog was originally bred to do influences the way it behaves. The American Kennel Club recognizes over 140 breeds, and there are hundreds more distinct breeds around the world. To make sense of the breeds, they are grouped according to their size or function. The AKC has seven groups:

1) Sporting, 2) Working,
3) Herding, 4) Hounds,
5) Terriers, 6) Toys,
7) Nonsporting

Can you name a breed from each group? Here's some help: (1) Golden Retriever; (2) Doberman Pinscher; (3) Collie; (4) Beagle; (5) Scottish Terrier; (6) Maltese; and (7) Dalmatian. All modern domestic dogs (*Canis familiaris*) are related, however different they look, and are all descended from *Canis lupus*, the gray wolf.

barking persistently can annoy and worry. A pack of Dachshunds giving tongue can be a formidable foe.

Naming the Dachshund

It is a commonly accepted fact that the name Dachshund(e) is German in origin and means "Badger Dog." Because the English presumed *hunde* meant "hound," the dog became a "Dachshund" minus the "e" instead of "Badger Dog" and ended up eventually in the Hound Group, though the breed was originally classified as a Working dog and then a Sporting dog by the AKC (though it was not used exclusively as a gun dog). The Dachshund does hunt on the scent like the Beagle and other scenthounds, but he also goes to earth and in that respect is an "earthdog" or "terrier."

There are many reference books that go into a much more detailed account of the Dachshund's development down through the centuries. They also mention the dogs and early breeders who helped make our present-day Dachshund. All of these books make fascinating reading.

Ch. Favorite v Marienlust, the most spectacular sire the breed has ever known.

The German revolution of 1848 put breeding dogs on the back burner, but the national foresters in all likelihood continued the practice because in 1879 Germany issued its first German Stud Book and made the first list of desirable characteristics of the breed. In 1888, the Teckel Klub (Dachshund Club) was founded. It set up its own stud book and tried to work out some arrangement with the Delegate Commission, but that never materialized. As a result, the Dachshund fancy began to split, since some dogs were listed in the Teckel Klub Book and some in the one maintained by the Delegate Commission.

19

Becoming Popular

Many local clubs formed all over Germany as the
Dachshund began to increase in popularity.

This gave rise to another so-called split. In 1895, many
breeders began to concern themselves with producing
dogs for the show ring and began to breed to that end.
These dogs increased the breed's size and also the
depth of chest. Some breeders felt such a goal was less-
ening the agility of the dog as a working hunter.

By 1895, the Dachshund came to be the largest entry
of any breed in the dog shows. This caused some problems with breeders, some of whom allowed the dog's
features to be exaggerated.

Also, to be registered in the German Stud Book,
any member of the Dachshund Club could make a
decision as to whether a dog should be included. And
most were, unless the animal was discovered to have

faults that made him
or her unsuitable for
breeding.

Later, it was permissi-
ble to register *any* dog
that was the offspring
of registered parents.
This practice affected
the quality of the dogs,

*1941 Ch. Max
of Hohenburg,
a wirehaired
dog.*

since conformation to the breed standard began to
play a far less important role. Two registered parents,
whatever their faults, were all that was needed to
ensure a place in the Stud Book.

Dr. Engelmann was one of those who was very instru-
mental in trying to change the new mentality, and in
1905 the "hunting dachshund" movement began.

In 1910, the German Hunting Dachshund Club was
formed. Breeders split according to their interest, and
the Delegate Commission tried to keep both groups
happy. Failing to do so, the commission lost its leader-
ship status.

The German Hunting Dachshund Club later, in an unselfish gesture, dissolved itself in order to create the Federation of German Working Dachshund Clubs. It was this federation that set up the standard for working Dachshunds.

In 1905, a club for the Breeding of the Miniature Dachshund was formed, but after ten years of unsuccessfully trying to develop true Dachshund type that would consistently produce the small dog they desired, they disbanded. That same year, Forester Kroepelin had a kennel of small Dachshunds and formed a new club—The Miniature Dachshund Club.

At this point, each nationally organized club maintained and published its own stud book. The only one, however, who did more than simply register pedigrees was the Working Dachshund Club, which listed only those dogs that passed certain tests set up by the federation.

It is widely accepted that the smooth variety was first on the scene. According to Herman Cox, noted Dachshund breeder and judge, the first wirehair appeared in 1812, though he does mention in his book *Cox on Dachshunds* that "in 1836, some sixty years before the three varieties reached their popularity in Germany, Dr. Reichbach included in his discussion portraits of all three varieties."

The longhair appeared to be around in 1820 but did not reach the show ring until 1882, when a longhair owned by a Captain v. Brieman of Bernberg was shown. The captain had been breeding that variety since 1874, and when the standard for the longhair was written in 1882, it was the captain's dog that they used as a model.

In 1909, in order to bring all independent clubs together, one club was formed and called itself the Association of German Working Dachshund Clubs. This served to unify breeders, and they worked together until World War I.

England played a vital part in the Dachshund's history by writing the first standard of perfection for the breed. It was abandoned in 1907, however, when the English adopted the German standard, since over the years, the English breeders had developed great respect for the Dachshund coming out of Germany.

Twentieth-Century Hounds

By the early 1900s the Dachshund breeders of the years before finally were able to produce dogs who were relatively free of the major faults the breed had been plagued with up to that point. In 1911, 1912 and 1913, respectively, the lines that became the backbone of our present-day Dachshund evolved: The Flottenberg prefix, bred by G. F. Muller (1911), the Lindenbuhl prefix, bred by Simon Barthel (1912), and the Luilpoldsheim prefix bred by Emil Sensenbienner (1913).

In the beginning, the Dachshund came to America in three ways—with the military who found the breed appealing and returned home with one in tow; with those wealthy enough to travel abroad and return with breeding and show stock; and with those who emigrated to America and promoted the breed.

One of those who imported excellent stock from Germany was a man by the name of Herbert Bertrands, who with his wife, Ellen, established the famous Ellenbert Kennels. The Flottenberg dogs appealed to them, so they imported stock from this German kennel regularly.

Herbert Sanborn also played an important role in those early years. Having studied in Germany in the early 1900s, he showed his dogs in Europe before he brought them to the United States and was able to continue their show careers and use them as breeding stock for his Isartal foundation dogs.

There were a few people, however, who were the backbone of the American breeding program, and they were also the guiding spirits of the Dachshund Club of America: Harry Peters, Sr.; G. Muss-Arnolt, an artist; and Dr. Montebacher, a doctor and chemist.

Interestingly, Dr. Montebacher kenneled his dogs in his drugstore, under the shelves! When he died, his dogs went to Mr. Peters, and since Dr. Montebacher was interested in dapple Dachshunds, when Mr. Peters took over his dogs he had among them some of the "tiger" Dachshunds, as they were then known. It was Mr. Peters, Sr., who was therefore to make history by showing the first dapple Dachshunds in this country. It was also Mr. Peters Sr. who became the first president of the Dachshund Club of America.

Hunting Dachshunds out for a walk.

The person, however, whom many credit with holding the breed and the Dachshund Club of America together, and who continued to operate her kennel during those trying years of WWI, was Mrs. C. Davies Tainter of Voewood fame.

The AKC remained firm in its stand that they did not want six Dachshunds in the Hound Group, and while there are proponents of this theory, even today, the stand taken all those years ago by the AKC remains unchanged. However, one thing has changed. The Miniature Dachshund no longer is considered the "step child" of his Standard counterpart! This is thanks to the many breeders of Miniature Dachshunds down through the years who have worked hard and have made continuous improvement in all three varieties of the breed.

One cannot talk about Dachshunds in America without mentioning Fred and Rose Heying and their contribution to the breed. They lived in California and had been breeding since the 1920s, but it was in 1945 that the Heyings purchased a dog from the Josef and Marie Mehrers' Marienlust Kennels. Josef had named that puppy Favorite, and he was shown as Favorite v Marienlust.

It is impossible to measure the impact that the Heyings' dog Favorite made upon the breed. He is behind most of the smooth Dachshunds in America, and at the time of his death, he had ninety-five champions. His sons and his daughters carried on his legacy, and the Heyings developed a strong line founded upon this handsome black and tan Standard.

Not only the Heyings, but many of the breeders of that time founded their kennels on the Marienlust stock. Josef and Marie were knowledgeable, and Josef was an astute breeder and had the knack of knowing what sires and dams clicked.

Dachshunds were bred to work above and below ground.

Another breeder, Mr. John Cook (who was later known as "Mr. Dachshund"), began his famous Kleetal strain of smooth Standards. His kennels were extensive and his knowledge of the breed likewise. It is impossible to include all of the kennels and people who made such an active contribution to make this little hound an ever-popular resident in the dog world. For those of you who want to investigate more of his history, please refer to the books listed on page 35.

In the Limelight

Because of the adaptability of this little hound who thinks big and has such an alert, intelligent outlook on life, the Dachshund has had his share of the "good life."

The Ugly Dachshund, a Walt Disney film available on video, shows how three or four of these hounds take charge of one Great Dane, causing havoc along the way.

Another Miniature Dachshund was a major player in Tom Wolf's novel *The Bonfires Of The Vanities,* and appeared in the movie role. In *Once Upon a Crime,* starring the late John Candy, two red smooth Dachshunds add a touch of comic relief and are a major part of the plot.

Hollywood has always been partial to this congenial, intelligent hound. Errol Flynn, Clark Gable, John Wayne, William Randolph Hearst, Andy Warhol, Paulette Goddard and Carol Lombard all fell for this long little dog with the short legs and the merry heart.

Pablo Picasso, Sir Noel Coward, columnist Liz Smith, the noted archeologist Iris Love and famed photographer Sidney Stafford have claimed these hounds for their own.

As you can see, the Dachshund has survived through the centuries due to the dedication of the many breeders and owners who persevered to make this dog what he is today. He is used successfully in the field; he is at home in the show ring, where he does a great deal of winning in all coats and both sizes; and he is active in the obedience ring. He competes in den trials as well as field trials, and it does seem that the strife of earlier times, which split the breed into two sectors— field and showring—has found common ground. It is not uncommon for a dog to do both. There are many dual champions.

**FAMOUS
OWNERS OF
DACHSHUNDS**

Pablo Picasso

John Wayne

Clark Gable

Andy Warhol

Paulette
Goddard

Liz Smith

E. B. White

Errol Flynn

Carol
Lombard

William
Randolph
Hearst

chapter 3

The **World**
According to the
Dachshund

This is perhaps a very apropos title for a chapter on how the Dachshund relates—there is only one world . . . his world! He honestly believes he is the principle player, and he acts accordingly. We don't own him, he owns us! He would prefer to act as a dictator but will surrender power for a piece of cheese, a walk or a ride in the car.

He is interested in *everything!* If he feigns indifference, don't believe him! He does nothing halfheartedly, and since he feels he owns you, he very much wants to be a part of you and make your world his.

The Dachshund is not a quiet addition to a home: she wants to be with you! Anywhere you go, she will go; any place you sit will be just perfect for her; anything you're eating will be fine, thank you! She is comical without planning to be, protective when she feels she needs to be and solicitous when she senses things are not quite right in your world. Her world, however, is fine as long as you are in it!

Expect the Unexpected

What can you expect from this alert little hound? The unexpected! Remembering he is a scent hound will save you a lot of aggravation. His nose is extraordinary! Someone once said he can smell a half a teaspoon of salt in gallons of water. Awesome! While this may not be an accurate statement, it's pretty close. Dachshunds can smell paper-towel towel tubes in a wastepaper basket, a speck of food under a cabinet, a crumb, well aged, behind the refrigerator! If he tells you something is lurking beyond your sight, believe him!

This delightful little hound is, however, a dichotomy.

While she keeps you guessing and will always surprise you, she is predictable and single-minded. What she likes, she will always

Dachshunds are interested in everything.

like; habits once ingrained, stick. However, she has a mind of her own, and she uses it. As mentioned in Chapter 1, she will outsmart you with great glee anytime the chance arises.

My first Dachshund, Whisper Hill's Walkin' Happy, went reluctantly to obedience school. We trained together and she worked well. My handler took her to Bermuda to try for the first leg on her CD (Companion Dog) title.

"Liten" had a lark; my handler was mortified—not once but every day! The first day, the spectators were minimal. Liten pranced into the ring, listened to the command to "heel" and moved out—not at Jane's left side but straight to the judge's table, out of the sun, while Jane had to move slowly, normally and quickly, stopping when told so that her "companion" dog could sit at her left side. Liten sat, all right—watching the whole exercise in the shade. The other exercises she performed like a pro!

CHARACTERISTICS OF THE DACHSHUND

Curious

Agile

Single-minded

Comical

Fearless

Sturdy

Scent hunter

The next day, having reviewed the heeling exercise, Jane confidently entered the ring, feeling they had it made. Liten heeled to perfection! But on the recall, she ran toward Jane—and kept on running, straight into the lap of a child sitting in the grass eating an ice-cream cone! By the third day, spectators were two deep around the obedience ring, anxious to see what the Dachshund had in mind this time.

The heeling was perfect; the recall was executed with speed and accuracy. During the long "down and stay," Liten almost made it. But at the last minute, before anyone could remove her so she wouldn't distract the other dogs, she had slipped under the rope and stood by a man eating, of all things, a hot dog!

On the makeup day, Jane thought there wasn't anything more Liten could do to embarrass her and decided to chance it. By this time, ringside was very crowded. Liten had become a star attraction! She sailed through all the things she messed up on the preceding days and then, after the long down, when the exercise was over, she did a perfect recall on the come—but kept on going and waited for Jane outside the ring!

Liten knew what she was doing. She enjoyed the attention of the crowd. She basked in her reputation for failing each day—for a *different* command! She was always her own dog, and she *never* disobeyed a command outside the obedience ring until the day she died, three weeks shy of her sixteenth birthday.

She was my first Dachshund and was only an interim dog until I could get another Collie. But living with her pushed all other breeds out of my mind and my heart. She was a challenge and a baptism of fire. I knew nothing of the things I will share with you in the following chapters! She destroyed my sofa and assorted chairs, ate the books in my bookcases one by one, but *only* the back two or three pages—never the covers! She slept on the bed, under the blankets, and until she grew too old to hear, no one could approach my bed, except children, while I slept.

So, what can you expect from your Dachshund? Loyalty. Love. Humor. Agility. Curiosity. Intelligence. Some think they are spiteful, but I honestly believe that dogs do not think as we do and live in an ever-present "now."

A Hunting Hound

The breed hunts—anything. Scents appeal to him. That's what he was bred to do. So, off he will go, following a scent—most likely your scent—straight to your shoes or your clothes or your mattress or to food!

His curiosity can get the Dachshund in trouble.

Believe me, it is much easier to keep things away from him than to keep him away from things! Remember that. It will save you a lot of aggravation and a lot of money!

Because this breed is so curious, it is easy for them to get into trouble. They don't worry or wonder what something is or how it tastes—they investigate! They have strong jaws, strong teeth, strong opinions, and strong hindquarters. They are agile and can jump—or at least try. If they can't get up on a chair or a table or a bed, they can use their teeth and their ability to bounce like a jumping jack and grab hold!

I know one who ate right through a linoleum floor because someone had spilled gravy on it. Years ago, Liten ate the pocket out of an expensive jacket draped casually over a chair, to get to a few pieces of dried liver. My Whisper Hill's Merry Mint will be two this year, but I will *not* leave her alone in *any* room unless I pull *all* chairs and tables out of her reach! She is loving and lovely, but she is young and active and curious! She knows no fear, and she doesn't hear very well!

Dachshunds love toys and balls.

The Dachshund is a hunter and will hunt. Perhaps not scientifically but naturally. Because she is a scent hound, it is difficult to keep her nose from the grass. Summer shows present a problem if they are held outdoors, and many obedience people prefer the fall and winter shows held on cement floors. However, in the conformation ring, a minute piece of liver will pull that head and nose to the floor in a second!

Yet, as active as this hound is, she is a lapdog, a sleep-next-to-you-in-the-chair dog, a curl-up-at-your-feet-in-the-bed dog.

The Dachshund is also a sturdy dog. Even the Miniature is not a fragile animal. Small is not a word in the Dachshund's vocabulary.

This hound is also persistent. He'll bark at the garbage until you remove it. He will jump on the furniture no matter how many times you tell him *"No!"*—unless you remain firm and do not give in. Being opinionated, he will test you. Being sly, he will do it if he thinks you're not around. Being intelligent, he will get down when he hears you coming or if you are forceful in your command to "Get off the sofa!" To be honest, it is easier to cover the chair or the sofa or keep him out of any room you don't want him to claim as his own. Believe it or not, some do prefer the floor. I have a few who lie by my feet or under my chair. Others won't have enough leg under them to make the jump onto furniture without a footstool or a helping hand.

Quick, Playful, Hungry!

Despite the jokes made about her shape, the Dachshund is quick and agile. Chasing and running after her is a no-win situation! Standing still is good, because if you feign interest in something, her curiosity will eventually win out and she'll give up the cat-and-mouse game and come to investigate. Hopefully!

This little dog loves toys and balls and paper-towel tubes and will amuse herself for hours if her people won't play with her. Many will retrieve but will not necessarily surrender. It is not good to engage in a tug of war with her. Her jaws are strong, and so are her teeth. Pulling against her, you can lift her off the floor and she will not let go. It is not good to let her realize the power of those teeth.

Expect your Dachshund to beg if you don't train him not to do so. He is a chowhound, and more often than not he will eat anything. He will steal, given the chance, and be a pest if allowed. Ban him from the kitchen or dining room until you have trained him to stay away from the table. "Stay!" is a good command to teach early!

As I said before, don't let him do once what you don't want him to do forever! He can melt your heart with those eyes. You have to steel yourself against him.

A DOG'S SENSES

Sight: With their eyes located farther apart than ours, dogs can detect movement at a greater distance than we can, but they can't see as well up close. They can also see better in less light, but they can't distinguish many colors.

Sound: Dogs can hear about four times better than we can, and they can hear high-pitched sounds especially well. Their ancestors, the wolves, howled to let other wolves know where they were; our dogs do the same, but they have a wider range of vocalizations, including barks, whimpers, moans and whines.

Smell: A dog's nose is his greatest sensory organ. His sense of smell is so great he can follow a trail that's weeks old, detect odors diluted to one-millionth the concentration we'd need to notice them, even sniff out a person under water!

Taste: Dogs have fewer taste buds than we do, so they're likelier to try anything—and usually do, which is why it's especially important for their owners to monitor their food intake. Dogs are omnivores, which means they eat meat as well as vegetable matter like grasses and weeds.

Touch: Dogs are social animals and love to be petted, groomed and played with.

31

The Dachshund is not normally a one-man dog, though she may prefer some family members over others. A well-bred Dachshund's temperament is cordial and outgoing. She is slightly wary of strangers and makes an excellent watchdog. Properly introduced to children, she accepts them willingly and makes an ideal companion for them. Common sense is the secret here. Children who are young should be supervised; older children should be educated in the proper and considerate ways of handling a dog.

Dachshunds are devoted to their owners.

Never forget your Dachshund is a scent hunter and should *never* be off leash unless she has thorough obedience training. Once she gets the scent, she is single-minded and will be off. Off lead, this hound, in almost any instance, is not trustworthy unless trained to respond to your verbal or signaled commands. She may stay by your side or never leave your property nine times out of ten, but she is not by nature a stay-at-home dog; if she picks up a scent, she'll track it!

The Dachshund is also a pack dog and loves his own kind. He can be tolerant of cats if introduced properly or if he grows up with them in the family. Other people's cats are a toss-up!

Hamster and rabbits are natural prey to him and should *never* be on the same level, loose or caged, with this hound.

Because he hunts on the move, young children need to be taught not to run away from this dog, especially while making loud noises! His natural instinct may cause him to give chase. Running by his side or behind him is totally different and should cause no problems.

It will be up to you to make sure guests who are welcomed to your home are introduced to your

Dachshund. She is an alert watchdog and needs to be told it is all right for this person to come into her domain.

Well-bred Dachshunds are happy-go-lucky and want to get into anyone's lap! Non-dog people may not appreciate that! While not happy about this, your Dachshund should respect their feelings even if she doesn't understand them!

A puppy who has been properly socialized will make a gentle, loving companion who will readily accept anyone you accept.

Be careful that your dog does not slip out the door while you are greeting guests, as he might take off unless he has been trained.

The Dachshund loves high places! And he loves to see what is going on around him. He is very rarely a sideliner, a bystander, a wallflower! What goes on on his front lawn, his street, next door or down the block is part of his territory. He watches and he listens and he barks! Persistent training will curb this, but no one will sneak up on you unawares!

Dachshunds are agile, hearty workers.

This lively hound is not an outdoors-only dog. Tied up, she will bark her head off. She will gnaw through any rope, and left out for long periods in a fenced area, she will dig her way under! (More about that in Chapter 4.)

A Faithful Companion

The Dachshund is a people dog! She'll stay where you are and go where you go. She wants to be with you. Should you get absorbed in painting the lawn furniture or planting bulbs, she may become bored and wander off, so make sure you keep an eye on her whereabouts!

33

When she is with you, she will be content. If she knows you're coming back, she will wait patiently. But she won't be the kind of dog you can pat on the head and then leave to go off and do other things. She will demand her share of your attention, and she will delight you with the warmth of her welcome.

The Dachshund is a clean dog, easily housebroken if trained with praise and encouragement. As a breed, they want to please you and don't respond readily to harsh methods.

The coat is easily maintained, with the longhairs and the soft-coated wires needing more attention than the smooths and wires with the correct rough coat.

Once trained to walk on the lead, until age slows him down, this alert inquisitive hound loves walks and hikes through the woods, around the neighborhood or down the street. Remember, *always* on the leash unless trained to obey the basic commands.

Are there down sides? Of course, the Dachshund is active. She can be strong willed, if you allow it. Bored, she can get into mischief. She loves to dig holes and will frustrate a gardener, but this can be controlled. She loves to burrow under blankets and under anything you put on the chair to protect the upholstery. If you allow her to share your bed, no matter now large it is, you'll find yourself curled up near the edge as she spreads out under the covers!

Once you are owned by a Dachshund, you will never come into a room or a house you've left, even if it was only to take out the garbage or bring in the newspaper, without this delightful little hound greeting you with his tail beating the floor, so delighted to see you, so happy you've returned to his world.

Having lived with this breed for nearly thirty years, I can assure you that there's no dog like this dog. No companion as comical, as loving or as adaptable. His goal in life is to love you, protect you and be your very best friend.

MORE INFORMATION ON DACHSHUNDS

NATIONAL BREED CLUB

The Dachshund Club of America, Inc.
Mr. Walter M. Jones, Secretary
390 Eminence Pike
Shelbyville, KY 40065

The club can give you information on all aspects of the breed, including the names and addresses of local breed, obedience, field trial and terrier trial clubs. Inquire about membership.

BOOKS

Fiedelmeier, Leni. *Dachshunds, A Complete Pet Owner's Manual.* Hauppauge, N.Y.: Barron's Educational Series, 1984.

Meistrell, Lois. *The New Dachshund.* New York: Howell Book House, 1976.

Nicholas, Anna Katherine. *The Dachshund.* Neptune, N.J.: TFH Publications, 1987.

MAGAZINES

The Dachshund Review. Hoflin Publishing, Inc., 4401 Zephyr Street, Wheat Ridge, CO. 80033-3299.

VIDEOS

American Kennel Club. *Dachshunds.*

Living

with a

part two

Dachshund

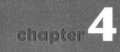
Bringing your
Dachshund
Home

Now the adventure begins! Hopefully you and your Dachshund puppy will have a relationship spanning ten or fifteen years or more.

Do not feel your puppy is being deprived if you have to leave him home alone! There are ways to handle all situations. Until recently I taught full time and raised litters and young puppies with no adverse complications. Most of the breeders I know also have full-time jobs away from the home. In today's economic environment, working families are the norm. It's quality time that's important.

A Place for Your Puppy

Usually, the best place for a young puppy is in the kitchen, especially if it is not carpeted. Make sure all wires, cords and cables are well out of reach, and block off the doorways with sturdy gates. Be sure your puppy won't be able to slip underneath or through them. The mesh ones are more practical; the ones you pull across will not contain a young puppy. She can slip through the wide spaces easily. There are many gates on the market today, and some even unlatch and allow you to pass through and still keep the puppy confined.

If the puppy will be free in the kitchen, be certain there is nothing on low shelves she can get into and no spaces between or behind cabinets or appliances where she could conceivably get stuck! Remember, the Dachshund is *curious!* Make certain, if you have children, that toys or pieces of games or puzzles are out of reach! Puppies put everything into their mouths! Also, make sure there are no poisonous plants within reach. Cleaning supplies stored underneath cabinets that could be opened by an inquisitive nose, medicine, aerosol cans, tools and especially plastic garbage bags are potential hazards. Plastic bags can mean death to all animals and children—small pieces torn off can block their windpipes and cause suffocation. Also, make sure that garbage is out of the sight and smell of your Dachshund. They will, when older, knock over garbage cans and stick their noses in any reachable container unless the lid is tightly secured.

Using a Crate

I am a firm advocate of crates, but not the small types for such long periods of uninterrupted stays—especially for young puppies. Unless you have someone home or can have someone come in a few times a day to let him out to relieve himself and socialize with him for a while, a *small* crate is not advisable. Never lock a young puppy in a small crate for an entire day!

PUPPY ESSENTIALS

Your new puppy will need:

food bowl

water bowl

collar

leash

I. D. tag

bed

crate

toys

grooming supplies

There are larger crates and also self-contained puppy pens where the puppy can sleep on one side and still have room for newspapers at the other so he can relieve himself without soiling his bed. It is wise to have his crate open in the room when he's loose so he can become used to it. Leave a towel inside and his toys. He will go in and out at will and soon consider it "his." Then, when you close the door, he will be in a secure,

familiar place. It is a good idea to feed him in his crate and have time-outs in his crate. When he is an adult, he will always feel his crate is a haven.

There are also exercise pens that are portable, fold up and can be used outdoors. They are open ended and can be clipped with standard snap locks. You can enlarge them as your puppy requires more space. They make an excellent out-of-door confine-

Dachshunds are curious creatures—puppies especially!

ment area if your yard is not fenced. If you do have a fenced yard, these pens can be clipped to your existing chain link to set boundaries for your Dachshund if you do not want her to have the freedom of the entire area or have gardens you don't want dug up and rearranged! They also come in handy if you can't watch your puppy every minute and want to be sure she's safe.

The Dachshund does not do well staked out or tied, and no young puppy should be left out that way.

Leaving Your Puppy Home

On your first day back to work, unless someone is at home, make sure you allow extra time in the morning to take care of your puppy. If you go off in a rush, you may fret all day trying to remember whether you unplugged the toaster or put the garbage out of reach!

When you leave the house, it is wise to have a radio on, tuned to a talk or classical music station. The continuous voices will soothe your puppy and keep him company. Get into the habit of telling your puppy that he's to be a good dog and he's to stay, you'll be back. If you have time, warm up the car or put your bags inside, then pop back into the house to tell him he's a good boy. Repeat the "stay" command and the "I'll be back" phrase. In a very short time, he will then realize that you will indeed return. It is a good idea to tell your dog "stay" and "I'll be back" each time you leave the house, for whatever the reason. He will be learning what "stay" means and won't be trying to beat you out the door!

Give your new puppy a chance to explore her new home and relate to her new family, but *never* let her into any part of the house unattended, and keep her out of any room that is carpeted.

Make sure she gets rest times during the day, especially if there are children in the house. She will be the center of attention, and it will be easy to allow her to become too tired or too excited. It goes without saying that young children should be properly supervised anytime they are handling the puppy.

Make sure your pup has plenty of safe chew toys.

Your puppy should sleep in a warm, draft-free area. Although she is not crated during the day in a small place, you can crate her at night. In the beginning you may want to keep the crate in someone's bedroom. Should the puppy cry, they can reassure her. Try not to keep taking her out if she should com-

plain; this will teach her early on that if she makes a fuss, she'll get some extra attention. The Dachshund is a clean dog and really doesn't want to soil her bed. By the time she is nine or ten weeks old, she should be able to go through the night.

If you don't want to chance it, you can let her sleep where she spends her days until she is twelve weeks old. Then you can let her sleep either in her crate or in a bed in the kitchen. If you choose to have her sleep with you or some member of the family, be sure it's what you want, because once she becomes used to sharing your bed, she will not react with joy when you want to discontinue the practice! I know some people who allow their dog to share the bed while they are reading or watching television and then put him in the crate when the light goes out. As long as your Dachshund has a warm place to curl up and a blanket to burrow under, she will be content.

Bowls and Beds

Stainless-steel bowls or crock dishes are good and long-lasting; plastic of any sort is quickly chomped on by this breed. For some of these clever hounds, a weighted water bowl is advisable—some of them enjoy turning them over.

Also, bamboo beds or any other material but metal are not practical for this breed. These dogs *do* chew. They will also gnaw on the sides of their crates. In order to discourage this habit, you need a product called Bitter Apple. This comes in spray and cream form. Read the directions on each container to see which product fills your needs. I would advise you to have both the cream and the spray on hand and use either one as needed. It will save your life and your antique table legs and possibly your favorite chair! Either one of them will cause your Dachshund to back off. Just remember you must treat

HOUSEHOLD DANGERS

Curious puppies and inquisitive dogs get into trouble not because they are bad, but simply because they want to investigate the world around them. It's our job to protect our dogs from harmful substances, like the following:

IN THE HOUSE

cleaners, especially pine oil

perfumes, colognes, aftershaves

medications, vitamins

office and craft supplies

electric cords

chicken or turkey bones

chocolate

some house and garden plants, like ivy, oleander and poinsettia

IN THE GARAGE

antifreeze

garden supplies, like snail and slug bait, pesticides, fertilizers, mouse and rat poisons all four chair legs or the puppy will simply move on to the next one! You can use the spray on your toes as well!

When your puppy is young, after he eats and when he awakens, he will need to eliminate almost immediately. You will soon learn the signs—nose to the ground, sniffing and moving in circles. Try to anticipate this and get the puppy outside or to the paper. Leave the paper in the same place, and when you see the warning signs, tell your puppy to "go to the paper" or ask him, "Do you have to go out?" The Dachshund is intelligent and quick to learn. Take him to the same spot, using the same door, and with proper supervision your puppy should be housetrained with minimal setbacks.

You will learn when your puppy needs to go out.

Paper training comes in handy when the weather is severe, you are ill, your dog becomes old and can't wait eight or ten hours a day or if you live in a city and don't want to do an early-morning or late-evening jaunt around the block. (For more on housetraining, see Chapter 8.)

Distractions

Toys can be expensive but usually last. Your puppy, however, doesn't need many. Always get the latex ones, which, if torn apart, can be easily digested and pass without causing any blockage problems. Be careful, however, of the hard plastic end piece that keeps the squeaker inside! This can get caught in the dog's throat. Make sure that when one end has been worn down or the piece remaining is chewed so much that it is small enough to get stuck in the dog's throat, you take it away. I do not personally recommend rawhide because it breaks off in large pieces, and these can also get stuck in the throat or wedged between the dog's jaws so tightly she can't close her mouth.

Paper-towel tubes and toilet-tissue tubes are also great favorites with Dachshunds, who love to toss them around! Stay away from old slippers or discarded socks. Your dog can't discriminate between old and new! Nylon is also dangerous, so keep the panty hose and the knee-highs out of reach!

Marrow bones are great. I have a friend who, once the marrow is gone, fills the cavity with peanut butter, freezes it and presto—recycled bones that will keep your puppy busy for hours!

Collars and Tags

Any nylon collar is quite adequate for a young puppy. Make sure it isn't too small or too large. A young puppy balking against you can slip right out of a collar that

is too large for him and be off. A metal choke collar is really not necessary; even an adult Dachshund can be easily controlled by a nylon choke. Make sure it has enough play to release but not enough to drag when he is not attached to the leash; you want a two-to-three-finger excess, no more. Choke collars should never be left on your dog when he is alone. For around the house, I prefer a round leather collar or a nylon one. One of the reasons is that an I.D. tag can be riveted to the leather one or attached to the others.

Your puppy will love exploring your home.

Any six-foot lead is good—webbed or leather—if you want your puppy to have some roaming room. Should you want a shorter one, there are many on the market.

Take your pet with you and measure. Most pet supply stores will allow that. Retractable leads are popular today, but you don't have the power of an emergency "pull back and lift up" should you need immediate contact with your pet.

Your Dachshund loves to go with you, and she has endurance to spare—as an adult. Puppies should not be taken on long hikes or lengthy strolls around the neighborhood. They aren't good for her young, underdeveloped shoulders. Running free and romping is fine—in the house or a fenced area.

A youngster, of course, will need more frequent outings, but once she is a year old or more, a walk in the morning, one upon your return from work and another in the evening should do. If you have a fenced yard, your task is a little easier!

It is *vital* that your dog always wear some sort of I.D. The rabies tag alone is useless, since it can't be traced should your dog get lost. Your pet's I.D. tag should contain your pet's name as well as your name and phone number. The Dachshund Club of America has a rescue representative in almost every part of this country. If you lose your Dachshund, call the American Kennel Club and they can put you in touch with someone in your area (or the area where your Dachshund was lost) who will be only too willing to help you and get the word out to be on the lookout for your pet. (The address and phone number for the AKC are listed in Chapter 13.)

The best I.D. is a tattoo placed on the inner thigh of a hind leg. Most dogs are tattooed with their owner's social security number. Many dog breed clubs run

Puppies can live happily with other pets.

tattoo clinics. Check for one in your area. Your local veterinarian should be able to steer you in the right direction. It is a relatively painless procedure when done by a professional used to tattooing dogs.

There is also a microchip that can be painlessly inserted into the dog's muscle, between the shoulder blades. The drawback to this is that you need a scanner to read the chip, and if your dog is found by a person who does not know to do this, your pet might not be returned.

Always remember that, even if you have a fenced-in yard, your Dachshund loves a good walk, and taking him for a stroll each day is good exercise—for both of you. As your pet gets on in years, you may need to shorten the distance and slow down the pace, but even the old-timers enjoy new smells and a change of scenery.

Above all, do not be nervous, especially if this is your first puppy! Enjoy your Dachshund; be patient; treat him as friend; use your common sense; have your veterinarian's phone number handy and you'll be fine. Most of all, you'll have a friend who will keep you company, make you laugh and love you unconditionally for all the days of his life.

chapter 5

Feeding

your

Dachshund

One of the things you must remember when dealing with the Dachshund is that most of them will eat anything anytime anywhere! Over the years, I have had a few who walked away from their food dish with kibble left—but that's not the norm. More often than not, they will polish off their own meal and then try to con you out of much of yours! *Be firm!*

Many years ago, I was entertaining and had to pick up the groceries. I took the infamous Liten with me, and since I was in a hurry and preoccupied, I put the bags in the station wagon (way in the back!) and ran into the bakery to get the dessert. It had been pre-ordered and was ready, so I was gone but a few minutes. Yet, when I got back to the car, parked *right outside* the bakery door, she had

47

explored the groceries and selectively devoured five pounds of deli roast beef and half of the chopped chicken liver! She didn't even have the good grace to be sorry, never got sick and thought her throat was cut when I skipped her evening meal! As I said in Chapter 3, I learned a lot from Whisper Hill's Walkin' Happy! From then on, a barrier was installed and she never got within sniffing distance of anything edible in the car!

Finding the Right Food

There are many commercial dog foods on the market, so you have lots of choices. You need to choose one brand, however, and stay with it until your puppy transfers to the adult diet. It is not good to switch unless the product causes problems for your pet. All of them are probably more properly balanced and nutritionally sound than the food we eat!

Dachshunds have strong teeth and powerful jaws. They need the chewing action that a dry kibble provides.

Your young puppy should be on a food geared for dogs under a year of age. If your puppy's breeder told you what he had been raised on, or gave you a starter kit, it would be wise to continue with the same brand. Should you decide to switch, however, be sure to do so gradually, adding the new food to the other until you are feeding only the new diet.

HOW TO READ THE DOG FOOD LABEL

With so many choices on the market, how can you be sure you are feeding the right food for your dog? The information is all there on the label—if you know what you're looking for.

Look for the nutritional claim right up top. Is the food "100% nutritionally complete"? If so, it's for nearly all life stages; "growth and maintenance," on the other hand, is for early development; puppy foods are marked as such, as are foods for senior dogs.

Ingredients are listed in descending order by weight. The first three or four ingredients will tell you the bulk of what the food contains. Look for the highest-quality ingredients, like meats and grains, to be among them.

The Guaranteed Analysis tells you what levels of protein, fat, fiber and moisture are in the food, in that order. While these numbers are meaningful, they won't tell you much about the quality of the food. Nutritional value is in the dry matter, not the moisture content.

In many ways, seeing is believing. If your dog has bright eyes, a shiny coat, a good appetite and a good energy level, chances are his diet's fine. Your dog's breeder and your veterinarian are good sources of advice if you're still confused.

I prefer a premium, small-sized kibble for puppies, fed slightly moist and mixed with a small amount of meat and often cottage or ricotta cheese or some plain yogurt. When the puppies are a little older, I like to feed the kibble dry, adding extras to only one of the meals. When they are ready to go to their new homes, they are well used to the dry kibble and therefore will not turn up their noses if there are no additives.

I do not add vitamins because, as I have said, these foods are balanced and complete; however, if your veterinarian suggests your puppy or adult dog should have her diet supplemented, follow his or her advice.

Your puppy needs a food high in meat protein. Read the label before you make any decision, and select a product with a high percentage of crude protein from meat (30+) and a high percentage of crude fat (20+).

With the Dachshund, you don't need a lot of bulk, and if your dog is producing a lot of stool, she's losing nutrients. This is one of the benefits of a concentrated food—you feed less and more of it is absorbed, causing a reduction in stool.

Eating Habits

Dachshunds have a tendency to inhale their food, which may cause them to choke, so a mini-chunk or chunk pellet is best. If your dog eats too quickly, put a round flat stone (not pebbles) or an overturned glass or ceramic coaster with a rim in the center of his bowl. He will have to eat around it, and that will slow him down. Make sure it is large enough for him to push around but not to pick up and chew!

If your dog starts to heave because he ate too fast and you think he's in trouble, simply take the palms of your hands and press them gently against his rib cage on either side and apply slight pressure. If that doesn't work, cup his muzzle in your hand and blow gently into his nostrils. That will clear his air passages, and he will then be able to finish his meal. (An "old-timer" told me that years ago. It works!)

I feed my adults dry kibble and only add extras for bitches in whelp and nursing mothers. Some people feel that dogs are meat eaters and must have meat daily. That may be true, but I find that my dogs thrive just as well without a daily ration of meat. If you read the labels, you'll discover that many canned foods contain mostly filler and water. I do keep fresh chopped meat on hand, however, and store it in small bite-size balls to use as treats a few times each week with a dish of dry kibble. They love it but never turn their noses up when they're faced with a dish of dry kibble.

Should you choose to feed a canned food only, you may run into trouble with plaque or tooth decay, since the moist, wet food and those burger type semimoist foods do not give the chewing action necessary to keep teeth in good shape. Also, if your Dachshund eats soft food constantly, you'll have to provide crunchy treats daily, and you'll risk feeding too many snacks and a possible weight problem.

Should you really feel the need to add something to the kibble, try for a canned food with less filler and moisture content, or add some fresh vegetables or cottage cheese. Remember, everything your dog eats has to count as caloric intake, so if you give two or three bones a day, you have to adjust the amount of the kibble you feed her accordingly. Dachshunds should not carry extra weight. If you can see her ribs, she's too thin. If you are looking down on a dog whose midsection resembles a rotund oval or a basketball, she's too fat!!

Please make sure you never feed your Dachshund from the table. If you insist on giving table scraps, do it in

HOW MANY MEALS A DAY?

Individual dogs vary in how much they should eat to maintain a desired body weight—not too fat, but not too thin. Puppies need several meals a day, while older dogs may need only one. Determine how much food keeps your adult dog looking and feeling her best. Then decide how many meals you want to feed with that amount. Like us, most dogs love to eat, and offering two meals a day is more enjoyable for them. If you're worried about overfeeding, make sure you measure correctly and abstain from adding tidbits to the meals.

Whether you feed one or two meals, only leave your dog's food out for the amount of time it takes her to eat it—10 minutes, for example. Freefeeding (when food is available any time) and leisurely meals encourage picky eating. Don't worry if your dog doesn't finish all her dinner in the allotted time. She'll learn she should.

your dog's regular dish, with his regular meal. Always remember that your dog is not meant to be a "save the food from the garbage" excuse! You feel guilty about throwing away the leftovers, so you give them to Rover. Not good! You'll end up in no time with an obese Dachshund who will turn his nose up at his food because he knows you'll give him yours!

Ideally, your dog should not be around the table when you eat. You may want to crate him or feed him his meal at the same time, in his crate. If permitted, he can be an annoying part of the family meal and you don't want to deal with a begging dog for ten to fifteen years or more.

A Feeding Schedule

By the time you bring your puppy home, she will probably be at the stage where three meals will suffice. Morning, midday and evening. Should no one be home for the noon or midday meal, you may add a little more to the morning meal and the evening one. Puppies need to eat as much as they will eat. They will usually leave some food if they've had enough. If they polish off a meal, you're not feed-

ing them enough. Self-feeding is not good for puppies, since it makes housetraining difficult. They need to eat at scheduled times so you can be more certain when they need to eliminate.

Your puppy may let you know if you miss one of her mealtimes!

Fresh water should be available at all times, but try not to have either your puppy or your adult dog drink heavily immediately after he eats. I like to wait at least half an hour before I let my dogs out of their crates and let them drink. I also like to have them rest for at least half an hour if they have been romping or running before I feed them. I firmly believe it is not good for any dog to have strenuous activity before or after he eats.

I would strongly suggest that you feed your pet in his crate. When you eat your meal, he can eat his and then rest in his crate until your meal is finished. This will eliminate the begging problem entirely.

Puppies need a variety of chew toys.

Whether you feed in the morning or evening depends on your schedule. Most people prefer the evening when there's more time and less pressure, but that's up to you. For the alternate time, it is wise to give a dog biscuit or two to tide your Dachshund over. Raw carrots will do just as well. Be careful here; nothing from the table such as toast or eggs! If you insist, in his bowl, please, never from your hands!

Contrary to her human family, your dog does *not* need variety in her menu! The same food each day will not bore her. Changes in routine and constantly switching her food, on the other hand, may upset her. It is not a good idea to buy whatever happens to be on sale in the supermarket that week. By the time you get her gradually switched from one brand to the next, it will be time to change again. This will cause your dog digestive problems.

Your Dachshund is a creature of habit, and she likes her meals in the same place and at the same time, thank you! Should you forget her dinner hour, she'll remind you, have no fear! She'll even escort you to the cabinet or container where her food is stored.

Make sure her bowl is clean and that it is properly rinsed. A soapy residue will make her ill.

Some people feel that they can cook for their dog far better than any dog food company. Not so—at least today. You couldn't come anywhere near the nutritional value of the commercial foods. Adding to them may make you feel better but it isn't necessarily better for your dog. And by the time you add the oils and the fillers and the necessary vitamins, you'd be spending much more than you would on a bag of meal, and you'd be tied to the stove!

Adding Extras

Should your dog's coat become dry or lackluster, you may need to add some oil to his food. This sometimes happens in the winter when the heat is on and the humidity is low.

Some processed vegetable oil—two or three teaspoons a week—in his food will help. A little bacon grease will also help, but in these times when cutting grease and fat is paramount, you may not be frying. Cod liver oil will do and so will vitamin E.

Chocolate can be toxic to dogs even in small amounts and should never be anywhere near them. How toxic it can be depends on the size of the dog and the amount eaten, but it has and will continue to kill dogs who eat too much of it for their body weight. Please make sure that your children and your guests understand this also. Peanuts are not advisable for Dachshunds, and of course spicy foods and starch or fatty foods should be avoided. Also, if you're snacking, don't be a "good" guy and share! Let your dog snack on raw carrots cut into circles or manageable pieces.

TO SUPPLEMENT OR NOT TO SUPPLEMENT?

If you're feeding your dog a diet that's correct for her developmental stage and she's alert, healthy-looking and neither over- nor underweight, you don't need to add supplements. These include table scraps as well as vitamins and minerals. In fact, a growing puppy is in danger of developing musculoskeletal disorders by over-supplementation. If you have any concerns about the nutritional quality of the food you're feeding, discuss them with your veterinarian.

If you feel your puppy or your adult Dachshund is not thriving on her present diet, consult your veterinarian. Sometimes your puppy or adult dog may have parasites that require attention. A stool sample taken to your veterinarian will pinpoint those problems and you'll be given the proper medication.

There are three types of commercially available dog food—dry, canned and semimoist—and a huge assortment of treats (lucky dogs!) to feed your dog. Which should you choose?

Dry and canned foods contain similar ingredients. The primary difference between them is their moisture content. The moisture is not just water. It's blood and broth, too, the very things that dogs adore. So while canned food is more palatable, dry food is more economical, convenient and effective in controlling tartar buildup. Most owners feed a 25% canned/75% dry diet to give their dogs the benefit of both. Just be sure your dog is getting the nutrition he needs (you and your veterinarian can determine this).

Semimoist foods have the flavor dogs love and the convenience owners want. However, they tend to contain excessive amounts of artificial colors and preservatives.

Dog treats come in every size, shape and flavor imaginable, from organic cookies shaped like postmen to beefy chew sticks. Dogs seem to love them all, so enjoy the variety. Just be sure not to overindulge your dog. Factor treats into her regular meal sizes.

Like babies, however, sometimes puppies go off their feed. If they turn their nose up at a meal but show no sign of being physically ill, then wait until the next meal but keep an eye out for anything unusual. Sometimes teething can cause minor discomfort. If your puppy is still not interested in eating, consult your veterinarian. An adult Dachshund who refuses to eat is not the norm. Keep a watchful eye, and if you find she continues not to eat, consult your veterinarian.

As your pet gets on in years, there will be times when he won't want to eat. With an older dog, it is wise to consult with your veterinarian. Blood work and an exam may indicate a problem that needs to be controlled or cured by a special diet geared for specific ailments.

How much to feed is always difficult to determine. It depends on your dog. If I fed Jacob what I feed Mint, he would waddle his way through life. The best judge is your eye. Follow the directions on the bag for the weight of your dog, and then adjust as you see fit. Exercise is a variable, as is age. A sedate old-timer does not need what an active youngster does to maintain a good weight. When your adult dog reaches his golden years, it is often better to feed smaller amounts more often. Not more food, but the same food divided into small meals spread throughout the day.

You will find several books listed in Chapter 12 that deal with the care of the older pet. They will be very useful in the years to come in helping you meet the needs of the aging dog. Dachshunds can live long lives in relatively good health. In the past few years, I have had to put dogs down who were nearly twenty, and up until the very end they had only minor problems, which caused them almost no discomfort. I tell you no lie when I say they rarely missed a meal!

Using your common sense and consulting with your veterinarian will enable you to feed your Dachshund properly for all the stages of her life!

chapter 6

Grooming
your
Dachshund

The Dachshund is a low-main-
tenance dog and can usually be
groomed at home with relative
ease. If properly fed and exercised, the breed presents a
pleasing picture—compact,
neat, conditioned and athletic.
Therefore, you also want him
to be clean and well-groomed.
Naturally, the smooth is the
simplest variety to maintain on
a daily basis. Next would be the
correctly coated wirehair, then
the longhair and, lastly, the
soft-coated wire.

Basic Supplies

There are some general supplies you will need, regardless of the variety you own:

- bath mat
- shampoo and conditioner (specially formu-lated for dogs)
- rubbing alcohol
- soft-bristled toothbrush
- toothpaste (for dogs)
- canine nail clipper
- cotton balls
- flea comb
- ear-cleaning solution
- grooming table (optional)
- rubber mat (optional)

Unless your Dachshund comes into contact with some odiferous animal or rolls in something less than pleas-ant, frequent bathing is not necessary. It removes the natural oils from the skin and causes dander. And since the Dachshund normally does not have a "doggy" odor, she is usually pleasant to have around. So, use your discretion on how often you bathe your dog. Under normal conditions, I would sug-gest once every few months, but only if necessary. Of course in the summer when we ply them with flea sprays, you may want to do it more often. A good brush-ing session will do more to clean your dog's coat than soap and water, believe me! Also, and I will mention this often, never bathe your Dachshund *before* you groom her! Bathing is the last step in the process. And, since you need to groom your dog at least every other day, you certainly don't need to bathe her after *every* session!

Bathe your Dachshund after you groom him.

I will deal with generalities after we discuss specifics.

Grooming Your Smooth

So now, let's get to the smooth variety. Aside from the basic grooming necessities, what you want for your

smooth is some type of brush. I would suggest the
following: a rubber brush or a hound glove/mitt or
a natural-bristle brush (soft to medium). A comb is
really not necessary for the smooth, nor are the scissors
if your dog is not being shown. In the showring, the
whiskers are cut to present a cleaner line, but your pet
can keep his!

The more you stroke your smooth, the more you stimulate the natural oils of his skin, loosen the dead hair
and keep the coat's shine. So, while your Dachshund is
lying next to you on the floor or the sofa, you can kill
two birds with one stone: give him extra attention and
groom him at the same time!

*Smooth
Dachshunds
are the easiest
to groom.*

If you don't want to
use your hand, the
hound glove or mitt
is a good alternative.
It fits your hand like
a mitt (hence the
name) and has a
nubby surface on
the down side.
Rubbing this along
the smooth coat will
banish the loose hair
and stimulate the
natural oils.

If you prefer the brush, by all means use it. It accom-
plishes the same thing. So does the rubber one, which
is smaller, fits in the palm of your hand and has rows of
raised rubber stubs.

If you do this a little each day, your Dachshund won't
even realize she's being groomed and will sleep
through the whole procedure—especially if you begin
when she's a young puppy. She will then accept this as
part of her life. On the whole, most dogs don't like
grooming sessions and will hide when they see you
coming. So if you start when the puppy is still small
enough to sleep on your lap as you work, talking to her

in soothing tones and praising her as you go, it will be less of a battle as time goes on.

See how easy the smooth's upkeep is!

Grooming Your Longhair

It will be easier for you if I put the rough- or tight-coated wire and the soft-coated wire in the same section, so I'll slip the longhair in here. For her, you'll need more equipment:

- a pin brush
- blunt-edged (rounded) scissors
- tangle remover
- a fine- to medium-toothed comb

The longhaired coat needs more aggressive and frequent grooming than the smooth. If you don't work on her coat at least every other day, it will mat and tangle and your task will be unpleasant for your dog and a chore for you!

The pin brush is an efficient tool for this type of coat. It will go deep into the undercoat as well as the surface and help prevent tangling.

If you don't have a grooming table, use the floor. Have the dog lie on her side, and before you begin to brush, use your fingers to feel for mats or tangles, especially in the armpit area and in the feathering on the legs. There are products on the market that, when soaked into the tangles, will soften them so you can work them gently with your fingers. The longer the solution stays on them, the softer they should become. Please remember that combing them out before undoing them will cause your dog a great deal of discomfort.

Once you have brushed and combed out both sides and the feathering on all four legs, you'll need to deal with the tail and with her feet.

Taking the *blunt*-edged scissors, you need to trim around the edges of each foot and also between the toes. Dachshunds don't especially like having their feet handled, so you may need help grooming them.

When this is done, you'll need to have someone keep her standing and still. Then, holding her tail straight out from the base, you need to trim the underside of the tail so she won't soil herself when she defecates. Using the blunt-edged scissors, keep the tail extended with one hand and scissor with the other from the base out about an inch or more. Also, with the same scissors, go around the rectum about an inch or so in a circular manner as close as possible to the skin. Also, trim the fine hairs in the genital area (males) and the fine hairs around the vulva (females). These hairs should never be kept long, since they will mat and tangle and give off an odor if they catch the urine.

If you find these tasks unpleasant or are afraid you will harm your dog, have a professional groomer do them. Obviously, the dog must be kept still when you scissor these areas and the female needs to be standing.

When you use the brush or the comb on your longhair, go in the natural direction of the hair. You want the coat flat, not curled or wavy.

Grooming Your Wirehair

And now, last but not least, the wire coat. You'll need:

- a stripping comb
- blunt-edged scissors
- a pin brush
- a medium-toothed comb
- a hound glove
- thinning scissors

Just how tight your dog's coat is will determine what tools you'll need to use. A really rough- or tight-coated wire needs, like the smooth, minimal care. A stripping comb (never a razor-edged comb) is used gently down the back on a slant, to thin out the guard hairs. Never dig into the coat but skim on the angle. You're thinning, not cutting. How often do you need to do this? You'll know when you see the hair sticking up a little along his back, looking rather unkempt.

You can run a comb through his beard as often as needed to keep it from tangling, and you can use the thinning shears if the beard or eyebrows are too long or too thick. When you use the thinning shears, use short, quick motions. When you draw them away from the dog's beard, do it gently or you will pull hair and cause your dog some discomfort. (The blades on the thinning shears should be in the open position, which will allow you to remove the shears easily.) Since you're not grooming the dog for show, you can just as easily use the blunt-edged scissors on both the beard and the eyebrows, and you may feel more at ease with them than with the thinning type. It will also be necessary to trim the hairs around the genital area and around the vulva so they don't tangle if they become long enough. That will also depend on how tight the coat is.

The rest of the coat can be brushed with the pin brush or the hound mitt.

The soft-coated wire, in my opinion, should be taken down with the clippers by a professional groomer or a Dachshund breeder. The soft coat is fine and often long and will mat and tangle. It will require much daily maintenance and will be quite time-consuming.

The best thing in your favor is that wire breeders have worked so long and so hard to eliminate the soft wire coat that they are not as prevalent as they were once.

The longhaired Dachshund has special grooming needs.

A coat like this should be clipped several times a year, depending on the dog. Having it clipped during the summer months helps keep fleas and ticks under control.

If the dog came from a breeder, get some advice regarding coat care; perhaps someone will show you

how to clip your dog yourself. *Don't attempt to do this yourself if you have had no experience.* You could frighten your dog or injure her, and then grooming will be a terrifying ordeal for her for the rest of her life. Dogs do not readily take to the noise of the electric clippers, and if you're not careful to do it proficiently, the blade will overheat and you may burn the dog's skin.

This pretty much covers what each coat variety needs in the way of maintenance.

Should you decide that you would be better working with your Dachshund on a table, there are grooming tables that come with an arm attached so you can leash the dog

A well-groomed Dachshund is a lovely sight.

to keep him still. *Never leave your dog on the grooming table unattended (with or without the arm).* Should he decide to jump down, he could hurt himself. These tables have a rubber surface for firm footing, and they do save your back. They are sturdy, and they can be easily folded and stored when not in use. They also come in handy when you entertain, buffet style, with or without a cloth!

You can also use any table as long as it is steady and you provide a rubber or skidproof surface so your dog can have proper footing. However, unless your Dachshund has had obedience training and ample time to accept grooming, you may find the lack of a grooming table arm a problem.

Grooming Regardless of Coat Type

Now to the grooming, which must be done regardless of the coat variety of your Dachshund.

Routinely, you need to *check your dog's ears*—I would say at least once a week. Take a cotton ball dipped in alcohol and gently rub it around the inside of the ear. You also need to use an ear solution (there are many on the market) to loosen the wax buildup. Put a few drops into the inner ear and then gently rub the base of the outer ear between your thumb and index finger. This will help to loosen any wax; then you can take some cotton or a tissue, wrap it around your finger and gently remove the loosened wax; (Chapter 7 will deal with more serious ear problems).

You must *clip your dog's nails* regularly. As I mentioned before, the Dachshund is sensitive about her feet, and cutting nails can be a real challenge. The best way to handle this problem is to begin cutting your puppy's nails early on. Hold her on your lap and play with her feet. Handle them, stroke them, get her accustomed to having them touched. You can do this also while playing with her. Make sure you praise her often. Also, rub the nail clippers across her paws. Let her smell them, and feel them, all the while telling her they won't hurt her. Speak to her in soothing tones and gently take hold of her paw and barely tip the nail. Praise her lavishly and try not to let her pull away from you. Go slowly and stop before she starts to object. If she begins to pull away, correct her gently and do one more nail before you stop. At the end of each session, give her a treat.

When she grows, it may be easier for you if someone else holds her and you cut. If that doesn't work, switch.

You need only cut the tips of the nails off. It is difficult to see the quick on the Dachshund's nail. But if you misjudge and the nail bleeds, use a styptic powder to stop it. Place the powder on the nail, applying gentle pressure.

If you can't manage the nails yourself, have your veterinarian clip them. Nails that are too long throw the dog off balance and may cause back problems. Also, if the nail is too long, it will eventually turn inward, which makes it difficult to cut because of the proximity to the pad. If that is the case, let your veterinarian do it.

As far as *bathing* goes, when you do it, make sure that the dog has proper footing. And when you're finished, make sure your Dachshund can't get outside since, when freed, he will roll over and scratch his back!

Place cotton in his ears to prevent them from becoming waterlogged. With warm, never hot, water, using a hose attachment, soak his coat. Then lather him with whatever shampoo you want to use, starting from the base of the tail up toward the head. On the head, switch to a tear-free shampoo, if you're not already using one, to protect his eyes. When you've rubbed the soap gently through the coat, rinse him *well*! With the longs and the smooths you may want to use a conditioner or creme rinse, but do not do so with the tight-coated wire. You do not want a soft coat here.

Make sure you rinse your dog thoroughly.

When you are sure the soap is well rinsed out, towel dry your smooth briskly; your wire, with strokes going flat so as not to ruffle; your long, with the towel draped to keep the coat flat. You may use the blow-dryer on all coats if the dog is not afraid. If you choose to do so with the long-hair, brush the coat by pulling it away and then letting it fall flat against his side. You don't want the longhair to be fuzzy or curly. His fur should stay flat on the body, like that of an Irish Setter.

If you begin early, your dog will accept the blow-dryer. Be sure to dry the feet and between the toes of the smooth, particularly.

Using a Groomer

As with all things, use common sense when grooming, and if you feel you want it done professionally, don't think you're a failure! I must confess, I hate doing my dogs' nails and usually resort to breeder friends or my veterinarian, despite the teasing I get for being such a coward!

Ask your local veterinarian to recommend a reliable groomer in your area, or ask a friend who has a dog groomed where he or she has it done.

You may also visit a local dog show (minus your dog) and make an appointment with a breeder or a professional handler to see your dog in the near future and give you some advice. Most professional handlers groom and should be happy to help you or to recommend someone. Just don't ask them when they are busy preparing or showing their animals. Wander around the grooming tent and spot someone who seems to have already shown and is relaxing with a cup of coffee.

Most of all, if you purchased your dog from a local, reliable breeder, he or she will be a willing and eager resource for all the phases of your pet's life.

You want your Dachshund to look the way she was bred to look, even though she is not a show dog, and that includes her outward appearance. She is a smart-looking animal and deserves to be kept well-groomed. It will make her feel like she owns the world, and she does—at least her world and yours.

chapter 7

Keeping your
Dachshund
Healthy

In recent years all of us seem so much more aware of getting and staying healthy, of being more conscious of what to eat and how to avoid what is harmful to us and to our world.

The same attitude applies to your Dachshund's well-being. Prevention is the name of the game. An alert "catch it before it mushrooms" philosophy is just as important in dealing with him as it is when dealing with all the other aspects of your world.

Know Your Veterinarian

One of the first things any dog owner needs to do is establish a working relationship with a veterinarian. So, if you're never owned a dog before, you need to find a veterinarian you can trust. If you purchased your Dachshund from a reliable breeder, ask for a recommendation. Or, ask friends in the area who have or have had pets. You can call any veterinarian you are considering, make an appointment for your puppy's routine shot and follow your instincts. If the "vibes" are good, the staff is pleasant and the veterinarian is considerate, caring, approachable and someone you feel you can trust and work with, you can't ask for more than that.

When I had my Collies, I lived a distance from where I now live. There was a veterinarian not far from my house, so when I got my first Dachshund, I continued to use him until I moved to where I now live. There was a veterinarian clinic not three minutes from the new house, but I was skeptical and was willing to drive the distance to the other veterinarian. At that time I had Liten, who was then eight or nine, her daughter, Trina, and my first Miniature wirehaired puppy, Jenny, who was due for a routine puppy shot. So, I made an appointment at the nearby hospital and took her over. I figured there couldn't be too much of a risk with the puppy, but I wasn't trusting the "light of my life" to anyone new until I checked him out.

That was twenty years ago and not only Liten, who adored him, but every Dachshund I've bred, kept or sold has been treated by this veterinarian and his staff. Puppies who have started with him and are sold locally stay with him. I have never regretted my choice. The point is, always remember that if you're not satisfied you can go elsewhere. Your Dachshund deserves the best health care you can provide for him, so use your

WHEN TO CALL THE VET

In any emergency situation, you should call your veterinarian immediately. You can make the difference in your dog's life by staying as calm as possible when you call and by giving the doctor or the assistant as much information as possible before you leave for the clinic. That way, the vet will be able to take immediate, specific action to remedy your dog's situation.

Emergencies include acute abdominal pain, suspected poisoning, snakebite, burns, frostbite, shock, dehydration, abnormal vomiting or bleeding, and deep wounds. You are the best judge of your dog's health, as you live with and observe him every day. Don't hesitate to call your veterinarian if you suspect trouble.

instincts and common sense. Should you at any time need a second opinion on a serious matter, seek one with or without your veterinarian's approval. Any competent veterinarian would encourage or insist on such action. There are, as with people, specialists in all major fields of veterinary medicine. They should be consulted when necessary.

Dachshunds are prone to back problems.

Dachshunds and Disc Problems

One of the things I feel strongly about and will share with you is this: *Every* breed has some problem or problems; some have many. Dachshunds have a proclivity for disc problems. No Dachshund breeder who is reputable can deny that.

The Dachshund Club of America has done much to help define the problem, the cause, the treatment and the possible prevention by setting up a research fund. There is still a long way to go, but at least the journey has begun.

It was once widely believed that an animal built like this hound would be predisposed to problems. This theory was prevalent in the early years of the breed's development when the length of the back was exaggerated. Others thought trouble was inevitable if the rib cage did not extend back far enough to give proper support to the spine. Yet many long-backed, short-ribbed dogs have not been affected, and many compact dogs with ample ribbing for their length have. Some geneticists feel that the length of the back makes no difference. Today the thinking is quite different and quite varied.

Two theories, however, are becoming more universally accepted—that the disc problems are hereditary and that they usually manifest themselves between the ages of two to five years. Some people think that if the dog does not "go down" (lose the use of his front and/or back legs, even temporarily) during those years, he isn't likely to go down at all. But there are exceptions, so nobody can guarantee anything with regard to the disc syndrome. There is still so much we do not know. While the fact that it is a problem inherent in some lines would seem to make things easier, in reality, it doesn't.

Is it fair to blame the breeders? Not the first time. But only an unethical breeder would knowingly continue to breed from stock that has gone down. That doesn't do anyone any good—particularly the breed!

This is why it helps to know what lines are behind your Dachshund, and why it is more advisable to purchase your pet from a reputable breeder. However, if you didn't and you're not aware of your dog's background, don't despair. Many Dachshunds have the slipped disc syndrome. Many have gone down and lost the use of the hind legs, many have gone down in front, and many have died young because of this. *But*, many have gone down in the rear and in the front and have gone on to live happy lives with good medical attention and owners who carried through with dedicated care. Many more Dachshunds have had *no* disc trouble of *any* kind.

FIGHTING FLEAS

Remember, the fleas you see on your dog are only part of the problem—the smallest part! To rid your dog and home of fleas, you need to treat your dog *and* your home. Here's how:

• Identify where your pet(s) sleep. These are "hot spots."

• Clean your pets' bedding regularly by vacuuming and washing.

• Spray "hot spots" with a non-toxic, long-lasting flea larvicide.

• Treat outdoor "hot spots" with insecticide.

• Kill eggs on pets with a product containing insect growth regulators (IGRs).

• Kill fleas on pets per your veterinarian's recommendation.

I've been around this breed almost thirty years and have known very few dogs who have had to be put to sleep due to the disc syndrome. Some people reading this may have known or had two Dachshunds and lost them both to the disc syndrome!

Please remember that disc problems run the gamut from minor to major and often require only rest and medication. I had one Standard smooth who, one day when she was eight, could not use her hind legs. I panicked and ran to the veterinarian. He examined her and prescribed medication and strict crate rest for her for a week.

Though I had to carry her outside to relieve herself, she never lost control of her bodily functions. By the sixth day she was up and normal. She lived to be almost twelve and never had another bout.

Years later, I had a wire miniature who was extremely active. Abigal was always on the move, but when she was around four or five, she got bumped by another miniature while she was going down the dog ramp and came back inside in obvious pain.

When I took her to my vet, she indeed had a problem but it was very treatable. She never "went down," and with crate rest and medication, she was ready to track rabbits within two or three days. She did not lose the use of her legs. For the next six years, until I

A healthy Dachshund is an alert Dachshund.

lost her at twelve from something totally unrelated, she had two or three episodes, all mild, and responded to the treatment used previously.

Can you help your Dachshund avoid problems? Well, if it's in the line and you know it, you deal with what comes. Today the success rate with surgery is impressive on even severe cases. And many dogs have recovered quite well with acupuncture treatments and/or chiropractic adjustments. They may have to go for a series of treatments over a period of years, but they can lead a life of dignity and be relatively pain free and moderately active.

Homeopathic medicine is another treatment option for disc syndrome as well as other ailments. Worrying about whether your dog will have a disc problem is the same as worrying that tomorrow you'll have a car accident. If it happens, you deal with it as best you can. Meanwhile, you take precautionary measures. Try to keep your dog from climbing up and down steep stairs, especially if they are uncarpeted. Don't let her jump down from furniture to an uncarpeted floor. In fact, discourage her from jumping down at all. If you can't, provide a footstool or a small ramp, if possible. The Dachshund is quick, and you may not always be able to stop her before she jumps—but try.

You have to remember the Dachshund loves high places—they give him a better perspective on his world. Since when he's on his feet not too much happens at his eye level, he likes to be on top of things—physically and mentally! One can't run the world from the basement.

If your Dachshund sleeps on the bed with you, it would be wise to provide a carpeted ramp for her to go up and down.

An Ounce of Prevention . . .

To care for the overall health of your Dachshund, there are certain things you should have on hand—a dog-oriented first-aid kit, so to speak—kept within easy reach in case you need it. I would suggest that these supplies be kept separate from the grooming tools and not near your family's first-aid supplies. You don't want people to borrow from it if the other kit runs out of gauze or adhesive! But, just in case, check it periodically and replenish it

---

A FIRST-AID KIT

Keep a canine first-aid kit on hand for general care and emergencies. Check it periodically to make sure liquids haven't spilled or dried up, and replace medications and materials after they're used. Your kit should include:

Activated charcoal tablets

Adhesive tape
(1 and 2 inches wide)

Antibacterial ointment
(for skin and eyes)

Aspirin (buffered or enteric coated, *not* Ibuprofen)

Bandages: Gauze rolls (1 and 2 inches wide) and dressing pads

Cotton balls

Diarrhea medicine

Dosing syringe

Hydrogen peroxide (3%)

Petroleum jelly

Rectal thermometer

Rubber gloves

Rubbing alcohol

Scissors

Tourniquet

Towel

Tweezers

---

as necessary. (For what to stock, see the sidebar, "A First-Aid Kit.")

No one knows your dog better than you do, and sometimes your gut feelings will tell you something's not quite right. There are obvious signs such as vomiting and diarrhea, but sometimes your dog may have only an isolated bout of either or both, so these symptoms don't always mean your Dachshund is ill. However, if you notice he turns up his nose at a meal, is listless, is resting more or wants to be held and cuddled, has to go out more often or has accidents because he's caught by surprise, then you should take his temperature. This is the most reliable way to determine what to do next.

Use tweezers to remove ticks from your dog.

To take his temperature, lubricate the blunt end of the rectal thermometer and, holding the dog firmly (sometimes it's easier if the dog lies on his side), insert it gently into the rectum. Hold it steadily for at least three minutes.

The normal canine temperature ranges from 101 to 102.5°F. Should it be above that, contact your veterinarian. The first thing he'll want to know is whether the dog's temperature is up. When you reach the receptionist give all the necessary information, including the temperature. She will have to relay the message, as the veterinarian will most likely be with a patient or in surgery. Do not be upset if you are put on hold or told that the office or the doctor will get back to you shortly. Unless there are signs of serious distress, it is knowing whether your dog's temperature is above normal and by how much that will enable the doctor to determine what action to take.

Most vets are not prone to give diagnosis over the phone, so if the dog is exhibiting no evidence of dehydration or serious distress and there is no alarming rise in his temperature, he may have the receptionist tell you to watch your pet for an hour or so and then get back to him. Remember, it's your dog, and you always have the option of bringing your pet to the office to be seen.

After-Hours Care

If your Dachshund exhibits signs of distress after the normal office hours, call your veterinarian. Should you reach his answering service, they will tell you he is on call and have him beeped or they will refer you to whatever emergency clinic he uses.

These clinics open after normal veterinarian practices close and stay open all night until the other animal hospitals begin their normal hours. They also operate on weekends and holidays. Some veterinarians, especially when they have associates, handle their own emergencies, but smaller, one- or two-doctor practices often make use of the emergency clinics. Ask your veterinarian what his or her emergency procedures are before you need to use them!

It is a wise idea to drive to the emergency clinic some night when there's no emergency. Emergencies are no time to get directions when you are upset and certainly no time to get lost if your dog is in serious trouble.

These specks in your dog's fur mean he has fleas.

I lost a dog once, many years ago, because the vet had been dragged out four times that week in the middle of the night. The night I called to tell him I was on the way with an emergency, the vet was not at the office when I arrived because he had told his night man to call him when I got there. I sat in the waiting room in tears as my dog died in my arms, thank God not in pain. (There were no emergency clinics at that time.) In all likelihood, she would not have made it even had he been there, but because he had been called out for non-emergency treatments the other times, he wanted to be sure this time! I'm telling you this so you'll realize that an emergency is a *life-threatening* situation.

But I, too, made a serious mistake. I told the night man I was coming in and I came in. I gave no specifics about the dog's condition. I am not even sure I gave my name. I was upset and I wanted to get there in a hurry, so I was not thinking clearly, and it was my first emergency in the world of dogs. I will never forget it and I would never want it to happen to someone else with a first-time emergency.

Some of the many household substances harmful to your dog.

So, trust me! Once you have lived with your Dachshund, you will "know" when things are not right but bear watching, when she's in trouble and needs immediate care, when to wait, and when to pick her up and run for help. I knew my dog and I knew I had to run. I just ran too quickly and should have given the night man more information so the veterinarian could make a proper evaluation. Remember, the few minutes you spend speaking clearly and slowly to get the message across could indeed save your Dachshund's life.

I am not a veterinarian; these are merely some suggestions garnered from years of living with the Dachshund in all phases of his life—from his first breath to his last. When in doubt, consult your veterinarian immediately.

Common Problems

ANAL GLANDS

These are sacs located low down on each side of the rectum. They can become blocked.

Symptoms: Dog is constantly preoccupied with his rear; licking, rubbing himself along the floor, rug or grass. Emits an unpleasant odor—similar to a skunk odor.

Treatment: These glands are rather difficult to empty if you are not familiar with the breed and the exact location. And, if they are indeed blocked, the dog will not be too happy to have you try and try again! Best to let your veterinarian do them.

Cataracts (Clouded Eyes)

Treatment: If your dog is approaching his senior years, this is a natural condition. Usually this requires no treatment, just clearing obstacles that might cause him harm. If this condition is noticed in a young dog, seek veterinary care. A specialist may have to be consulted. Eye problems are not normally a concern in this breed, but anything can crop up.

Cysts

Can be found when you are petting or grooming your dog. Many older dogs develop these. That does not mean that your dog has cancer!

Treatment: Should you notice or feel a cyst with your hands when grooming or petting your dog, have your veterinarian check it, just to be sure. He will then advise you as to whether it should be watched (to see if it grows any larger) or if it should be biopsied. There is a high success rate for dogs who need to have cysts that are malignant removed. Of course, age and general good health also play a part here.

Run your hands regularly over your dog to feel for any injuries.

Diarrhea

Can be caused by sudden change in diet, parasites, digestive upset, or could be a sign of something serious.

Symptoms: Loose, runny stool; may or may not contain blood and/or mucus. Sporadic, uncontrolled bowel movements; sometimes bowels are moved at normal intervals but are loose.

Treatment: If it is not accompanied by any other symptoms, is not uncontrolled and is not continuous, treat with Imodium AD liquid. Check with veterinarian as to dosage per pound. Feed a bland diet of boiled rice and boiled chopped meat (small amount, to flavor, but drain off any grease.) If condition persists more than twenty-four hours, seek veterinary care.

DRY COAT

Squeeze eye ointment into the lower lid.

Symptoms: Itching; dander visible to the eye; lackluster appearance.

Treatment: A bath in a shampoo made for this condition. (Always use a *tear-free* shampoo on the head, near the eye region.) Shampoo from back to front, lather well and rinse well. Repeat in ten days *if needed.* Dry coat is more prevalent in the winter when the heat is on and the humidity is low. You can compensate for this by adding cod liver oil to the diet once or twice a week. Any oil, including vitamin E (break capsule and add to meal), will help. Also remember that bathing too much may also deplete the oil in the coat.

EAR MITES

Once called "canker," this is invisible to the naked eye and is contagious to other animals.

Symptoms: Constant pulling, scratching of ears; redness in ears; visible debris, usually black.

Treatment: Veterinary attention.

EYE DISCHARGE

This could range from debris in corner of the eye to constant tearing.

Treatment: Wipe away with tissue; if it seems colored or appears to be thick mucus, this requires veterinary care. On wirehairs or longhairs, check to see if there is hair too close to the corner of the eye; if this is the

case, pluck the hair out with your finger, having someone hold the dog's head still. If the hair is removed,
and the eye still discharges, seek veterinary care.

Genitals

There are a few things you need to
know here. The Dachshund is low
to the ground, and therefore the
females in particular can sometimes pick up urinary infections.
Males can get them from licking,
which causes pus to form in the
sheath.

Symptoms: Excess licking could be
because of a urinary tract infection.
Excessive urinating; attempts to urinate, producing small amounts or
nothing. Blood in urine. If the dog
is paper trained, small crystals are
visable when urine is dried.

Treatment: Urine sample to veterinarian. Males not intended for
breeding stock should be neutered.
Males with one or both testicles
undescended need to be neutered.

Spaying and Neutering

Most breeders sell their puppies
with a spay/neuter contract, so
unless you buy a show or breeding
prospect, the breeder expects your
pet to be neutered or spayed. Why?
Because there are too many surplus
puppies and too many animals sitting in shelters.

**ADVANTAGES OF
SPAY/NEUTER**

The greatest advantage of spaying
(for females) or neutering (for
males) your dog is that you are
guaranteed your dog will not produce puppies. There are too many
puppies already available for too
few homes. There are other
advantages as well.

ADVANTAGES OF SPAYING

No messy heats.

No "suitors" howling at your windows or waiting in your yard.

Decreased incidences of pyometra
(disease of the uterus) and breast
cancer.

ADVANTAGES OF NEUTERING

Lessens male aggressive and terri-
torial behaviors, but doesn't affect
the dog's personality. Behaviors
are often owner-induced, so neutering is not the only answer,
though it is a good start.

Prevents the need to roam in
search of bitches in season.

Decreased incidences of urogen-
ital diseases.

If you want a pet puppy for your family and you have
no intention of showing the puppy, he ought to be just
that—your pet—and should be neutered or spayed.
(Dogs may enter obedience classes in any dog show

even though they have been spayed or neutered.) It is really much better for the pet dog to be spayed, and it is certainly much more convenient for you!

The old wives' tale that every female should have at least one litter and every male should be a father holds no truth. Some feel that a female should go through the first season before she is spayed in order to fully develop. Check with your veterinarian to determine when he wants to perform the surgery. Being young, your puppy will bounce back rather quickly. You can normally take her home the next day.

If your male dog has only one testicle down in the scrotum, or has retained both testicles, it is important that they be located and removed. Therefore, the neutering of a male will sometimes become a little more involved if one or both of the testicles have been retained.

Playtime is a must for dogs.

The neutered and spayed Dachshund does not put on extra weight because of the procedure. Your Dachshund puts on weight because you feed him too much for his activity level—whatever that may be. There are three neutered males in this house; one is twelve and the other is ten. Neither one of them is overweight. There is a neutered male here also, and he is younger. Jacob could be overweight if I let him, but if I notice him getting a little too round, I cut his food back. Abigail was spayed after her first litter because of complications, but until she died at twelve, she never carried an extra pound.

HEARTWORM

This was not included with the other parasites (see below) because it is different in nature. Heartworm is transmitted by a mosquito that has bitten an infected dog and then bites your dog. The infection is passed through the bloodstream and can only be diagnosed through a blood test, which should be done *before* the dog is medicated. If your dog was put on preventative but did not remain on it, you must *not* start the preventative again without the dog being retested. If you have any doubt at all, depending on what preventative you use, contact your veterinarian. There is now a once-a-month preventative and many veterinarians are suggesting that the dogs remain on it all year. This means they do not have to be tested every year provided you do not stop the medication.

Puppies need to be tested before their first mosquito season and then put on the preventative. If you have used the medication during the season and discontinued it during the winter months, *do not* start again without retesting. This could prove *fatal.*

Symptoms: Breathing difficulties; loss of weight despite appetite; lack of energy.

Treatment: Remember, this is a *heart*worm and affects the heart, hence the breathing difficulties. Your veterinarian will do the blood test and dispense the medication. Most now favor the once-a-month dosage, and many suggest you continue it year-round. This medication can also be effective on other internal parasites. Depending on what area of the country you are in, your veterinarian will advise you as to the best procedure for your dog.

INTERNAL PARASITES

ROUNDWORMS
Usually found in puppies; transmitted by mother.

Symptoms: Pot belly, hungry but lackluster coat, sometimes runny eyes; can be seen by the naked eye; long and thin and continuous; may be seen in a spiral formation, resembling spaghetti.

Treatment: Any puppy wormer sold in pet stores. Follow directions carefully. Needs two doses ten days apart. Or take stool sample with worms to your veterinarian. He will then dispense the proper medication. Do whichever is more convenient for you.

TAPEWORMS

Caused by ingesting fleas, eating animal droppings (rabbits, etc., infested dogs), eating dirt contaminated with animal droppings.

Symptoms: Constant hunger even though eating well; seems thin despite amount of food; mucus in stool and sometimes blood; can be seen with naked eye—flat, white segments; do not however, appear in *all* stool. You may take a sample with or without the worms.

Treatment: Veterinary confirmation. You do not necessarily need to bring the dog, but you must know how much the dog weighs, so the proper dosage can be given. Follow your veterinarian's directions.

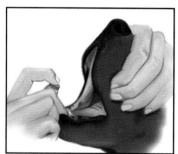

WHIPWORMS

These worms cannot be seen by the naked eye.

Symptoms: Blood in stool; mucus.

Treatment: Veterinary care. Follow same procedure as for tapeworms.

To give a pill, open the mouth wide, then drop it in the back of the throat

Since neither whipworms nor hookworms can be seen with the naked eye, it is best to have a stool check done at least every six months, especially if your dog is walked or exercised where other dogs also have access. Whipworm is picked up from contaminated ground.

LAMENESS

Can be caused by many things.

Symptoms: Limping; not putting a foot down; favoring one paw.

Treatment: Before you do anything, check your dog's paw or paws. Make sure you check between his toes. There may be burrs or pieces of pine cones, which are sticky and get lodged in paws, pads of feet and between toes. Carefully remove those with the tweezers. If there is a cut and it is not bleeding profusely, apply pressure until the bleeding stops, then put the foot on a gauze pad to fit. Wrap the pad with rolled gauze and secure with a gauze knot, not too tight. If you know from the start that it looks bad and the bleeding is profuse, go immediately to your veterinarian.

If the dog has pulled out a nail, which sometimes happens, it is very painful, and you need to make sure that it isn't dragging or hanging. If that is the case, then you need to him to the veterinarian because he will be in pain and most likely not want you playing with his foot. If it is a clean cut, use your styptic powder to stop the bleeding, and then have the veterinarian look at it. An open cut, even if it is not bleeding, can invite infection if the dog uses it without having a wrap.

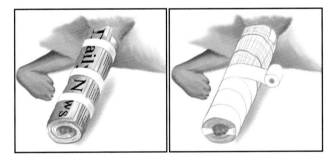

Make a temporary splint by wrapping the leg in firm casing, then bandaging it.

Lameness can also be caused by stepping on a wasp or if one or more of her nails are curling under. A veterinarian should handle nails that long. Also, if your dog has jumped down from the furniture, she may have pulled or sprained her shoulders and her leg. Crate rest is best for this. If the pain really bothers her, call your veterinarian and ask what you should use for pain. He may want you to bring the dog in if it still bothers her so he can X ray to determine the treatment. It goes without saying that you should not walk your Dachshund on hot pavements. This is not good for the pads of her feet, and puppies whose pads have not hardened could burn their feet.

Mange

There are two types of mange—demodectic (follicular) and sarcoptic. In both cases, dedicated treatment is absolutely essential. Sarcoptic is contagious and spreads easily. Demodectic is more difficult to cure and at one time could also be fatal.

Symptoms: Sarcoptic—unmistakable musty odor; itchy skin; hair loss; small pimplelike eruptions on head, around eyes and mouth; may appear on other parts of the body.

Demodectic—almost impossible to cure years ago, it is sometimes call red mange and may be detected in puppies between the three- to nine-month range. Many feel it is passed down from the mother. Same symptoms except red, raw, hairless spots appear all over the puppy.

Treatment: Mange can only be accurately detected by a veterinarian, who will do a scraping to study under the microscope. He will administer what is needed. As I mentioned before, dedicated treatment is absolutely essential.

Sparse Hair and Hot Spots

Symptoms: Loss of hair; small areas with no growth of hair. Can also happen if dog is biting or pulling at his coat or scratching.

Treatment: Apply vitamin E (break capsule) to spot and rub, or apply A&D Ointment to sparse places, or add more oil to the diet. Spray Bitter Apple on coat to discourage dog from biting or pulling it. If none of this works, or if the spots begin to ooze or run, your dog needs veterinary care.

Tooth Problems

Your Dachshund should not have any tooth problems while she is young and in her "teen" years. The only thing you need to check on is that all of the milk teeth come out. If you see that she has retained one or more, they need to be removed by your veterinarian in order that the adult teeth have the room to come down.

Symptoms: A dog with tooth problems will rub her muzzle along chair or sofa arms, the rug or the floor. Swelling can sometimes develop in the face area if a tooth is decaying or abscessed. Assuming that you do dental maintenance on your dog, bad breath can indicate tartar buildup. A bad tooth has a distinctive odor. With Dachshunds, refusing a meal is rare—I had a wire who never stopped eating and had bad breath; when I took her over to have her teeth cleaned, she lost fourteen!

Treatment: Polish your dog's teeth regularly during the young to middle years, and at least once every six months have your veterinarian check for tartar buildup. When your Dachshund reaches seven, it's time to have the teeth cleaned by your vet, if not sooner. Your dog has to go under for teeth cleaning, and the older he gets, the more of a risk that entails. I like to have dental cleaning done around age six to seven and then, if needed again, around ten. After that, I prefer that they not have surgery unless there is no way to avoid it. Hard biscuits and dry kibble will help. Brushing will help *a lot*!

Check your dog's teeth frequently and brush them regularly.

There are, of course, many other things that could crop up with regard to your Dachshund's health and well-being that, while not emergencies, need attention. I think I have covered the basic ailments in a manner that, hopefully, will give you guidelines. *Always remember that your veterinarian is the ultimate source, and should you run up against anything suspicious that gives you concern, make an appointment just to be on the safe side.* Some dogs do not exhibit the normal or expected symptoms.

Just recently a breeder friend told me her daughter's dog was exhibiting symptoms that both she and I felt were some sort of poisoning. We were both wrong. Her veterinarian said that for the first time in his many years of practice, he was seeing dogs that had symptoms resembling human flu, and this was what he felt this dog had. A sick, listless dog with trouble walking and in obvious pain so that she cried when she was touched, indeed had contracted what he felt was a flu bug! And so, as with people, since this dog was less than a year old, she was susceptible.

An Elizabethan collar keeps your dog from licking a fresh wound.

She had been a very sick pup, but within a day of the antibiotics geared to these symptoms, she was alert and willing to wag her tail and give kisses! I share this with you even though the dog was a Beagle and not a Dachshund, because anything can happen and virus strains can appear on the scene. This pup lives in a house with two older Dachshunds and under the watchful eye of people who know dogs. She had also been treated by a veterinarian for dehydration and given medication. Had her owner not reacted as she did when the pup got no better, she would have lost her. And if her regular veterinarian had not seen similar cases and changed the treatment, she indeed may not have survived.

Always remember that the young and the old need to be treated aggressively when they become seriously ill, and it is never a good idea to play the "waiting game" with young puppies or old-timers. Dachshunds between twelve months and eight years are pretty resilient and snap back more quickly.

Handling Emergencies

The following will deal with what I consider emergency situations. In most cases, as you will see, the only way to cope with most of them is to get to the nearest veterinary hospital or emergency clinic *immediately*.

You may never encounter some of the things mentioned in the following pages, but the unexpected and unprepared for events in our lives and in the lives of our Dachshunds can be handled far better by those who stay calm, use their common sense and react instinctively.

What to do if your Dachshund has an encounter with:

A SKUNK

The old remedy was tomato juice baths. Now you can also use a product called Massengill douche. You may have to repeat a few times to dispel the odor. I think you need to let the juice or the douche soak into the coat, but I would rinse it off, let the dog dry and then repeat as needed. An old-fashioned remedy that was effective was 25 percent cider vinegar to 75 percent tap water, but I think the Massengill is somewhat like that. If you don't want to bathe the dog, you can sponge the solution on, possibly outside or in the garage. Depending on where you live, your Dachshund may or may not ever encounter a skunk! What you need to watch here is your Dachshund's eyes. Spray in the eyes could be serious. Your veterinarian may have some ideas on the subject, and it would be wise to ask him what he would recommend if you live in an area where contact with skunks is possible.

A PORCUPINE

This may also be an unlikely situation for your Dachshund, but once again, you need to be prepared to respond. First of all, this encounter is potentially dangerous! The quills are painful, and my advice would be to get your dog to the nearest veterinarian as quickly as possible. She will be in pain, and there is no way you will be able to handle her and deal with the quills at the same time. In all likelihood, she will have them in, around or on her muzzle, and this is a *sensitive* area. You cannot muzzle her to protect yourself, and unless you have done this before and carry the necessary equipment, leave it to a professional.

A FISHHOOK

This is a potentially dangerous situation that will be painful for your Dachshund. If you do not have help and have not removed a fishhook from your dog before, don't attempt it. Because of the pain and the possibility of tearing the skin, I would strongly suggest you let the vet do it.

CHOKING

Obviously, if your Dachshund is choking you have to work *quickly*! Try to put your hand into his mouth and see if you can get the obstruction out. If this is not possible, hold the dog at a downward angle, possibly upside down, bracing his back, and shake gently while you pat his back. Hopefully, you will dislodge the obstruction. Since time may be of the essence, get your dog to the veterinarian's *posthaste*.

Applying abdominal thrusts can save a choking dog.

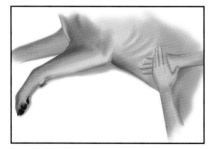

If I were you, I would discuss the possibilities of such a thing happening on a routine visit with your veterinarian. The toss-up between trying yourself or running for help is a judgment call you will have to make at that time. If it is of any reassurance, as I have mentioned before, I have been involved with this breed for many years and have had many dogs during that time, and have never run into this problem!

SHOCK (OFTEN DUE TO TRAUMA OR ACCIDENT)

If your Dachshund has a rapid, weak pulse, glassy eyes and slow capillary refill time (press finger against gums until white and then release and count the seconds until they return to pink), she may be in shock. The longer it takes to do this—three or more seconds—the more serious the condition.

Keep your dog warm and rush to the nearest veterinarian. *Do not attempt to handle this by yourself.*

A Car Injury

Should this happen to your Dachshund, the most important thing is that you be calm and act quickly.

1. Check for signs of *shock*.
2. Cover and keep the dog *warm*.
3. Try to keep the dog *extended*.
4. Make a muzzle with a tie, scarf, leash, whatever. A dog in pain may resist help by trying to bite.

To Make a Muzzle:

1. Make a loop in middle of scarf.
2. Slip it over muzzle.
3. Knot under dog's chin.
4. Pull it together.
5. Bring it back around his head, behind his ears.
6. Tie *lightly*.
7. Release *as soon as possible*.

Use a scarf or old hose to make a temporary muzzle, as shown.

Roll dog rather than lift onto a stretcher (made of a coat, blanket, etc.). Do the best you can, but don't linger. The sooner you can get to the vet, the better.

Should your Dachshund need:

Artificial Respiration

1. Check for *obstructions* in mouth.
2. Swab out *blood* or *mucus*.
3. Open mouth *slightly*.
4. Depress *tongue* with *one* hand, seal *nostrils* with other.

5. *Blow* into *mouth.*

6. *Watch* chest to see if it rises.

7. *Repeat* every *five* seconds, *ten to twelve breaths per minute.*

IDENTIFYING YOUR DOG

It's a terrible thing to think about, but your dog could somehow, someday, get lost or stolen. How would you get him back? Your best bet would be to have some form of identification on your dog. You can choose from a collar and tags, a tattoo, a microchip or a combination of these three.

Every dog should wear a buckle collar with identification tags. They are the quickest and easiest way for a stranger to identify your dog. It's best to inscribe the tags with your name and phone number; you don't need to include your dog's name.

There are two ways to permanently identify your dog. The first is a tattoo, placed on the inside of your dog's thigh. The tattoo should be your social security number or your dog's AKC registration number.

The second is a microchip, a rice-sized pellet that's inserted under the dog's skin at the base of the neck, between the shoulder blades. When a scanner is passed over the dog, it will beep, notifying the person that the dog has a chip. The scanner will then show a code, identifying the dog. Microchips are becoming more and more popular and are certainly the wave of the future.

HEATSTROKE

If your Dachshund is panting excessively and the weather is hot and humid, his panting becomes less and less effective. When this happens, you need to act *quickly:*

Pack in *ice* or

Wrap in *wet towel* or

Douse with *cool water.*

You *must* reduce the body temperature to 101.5°F!!! Once you do that, consult with your veterinarian!

It goes without saying that you must never exercise your dog in high temperatures or high humidity and *never* leave a dog in a car in the heat. This results in death very quickly! A car in the heat or humidity, even with windows opened slightly all around, will cause suffocation. So, even though your Dachshund loves to ride in the car, in summer heat it is wisest to leave him home! And when you do take him, leave someone in the car with him who could either take him out if he shows signs of stress or make sure that *all* the windows remain *wide open!* Even parked in the shade, the car will absorb the heat. If you are skeptical, park your car on a summer day, even in the shade, and roll up all the windows, or keep them cracked slightly, as you would if you left your dog alone. Then, just sit. If you don't get claustrophobic, it's a good way to appreciate how hot your Dachshund would become while waiting in a parked car for an errand that was to take "only a minute." And always remember that the black and tans always feel the heat more than the reds.

Please also use common sense when letting your Dachshund out in the hot and humid days of summer. It is best to exercise them in the cool of the morning or after the sun goes down. I always let my crew into the larger grassed area in early morning to stretch their legs and run off their energy, and then I close that yard off until the sun moves. For the rest of the day they can go in and out all they wish, but only in the smaller side yard where there is ample shade from a pine tree that sweeps the clouds.

Dogs acclimate to lack of air conditioning better than we do because they have sense to keep a low profile! Dachshunds are low to the floor, and since heat rises, they do better in summer when it's hot than in winter when it's cold and they can suffer from drafts. These dogs aren't stupid, and once they outgrow the no-sense puppy stage, they'll handle the heat *when* they are in control. They can, anyplace else, find the coolest spot. But, *in a locked car,* there aren't many places they can turn to in order to escape the heat radiating from the glass.

You may think it's sad when she gives you such forlorn looks when you say "no" to a drive when it's hot, but your dog is better off at home. Make up for that disappointment by taking her on a ride when you have no place to stop—except for a Dairy Queen, which you both can enjoy! It will relax you! You can also take her to Little League practice as long as she can sit with you in the grass and enjoy the action. And a crate-trained dog can go many places not open to one roaming free—I've often taken a dog with me to picnics or dinners and she remained crated and comfortable under a tree or in a family room, sleeping or gnawing on a marrow bone. (Always check with your host or hostess *before* you do that.) Once your circle of family and friends realize that the dog will not be a disruptive pest, I'm sure she will be welcomed.

Care of the Older Dog

Sometime down the line, your charming, always-getting-into-trouble puppy will become your canine senior citizen, so I thought it would be in your Dachshund's best interest to talk about the senior years.

It is commonly felt by most breeders that every year after ten is a grace period. It is then that you need to develop a more vigilant eye and make changes as your Dachshund ages, to make his days more comfortable and enjoyable.

Like us, they end where they began—sleeping more, needing to go out more, forgetting sometimes where they were heading and why, wanting to eat more often and very much needing reassurance and the security of our love.

It is easy to become impatient with our old-timers. They can be demanding. They want what they want *now.* Just a few suggestions:

Sometimes bringing in a younger companion will add years to an old-timer's life. Not a very young puppy but one old enough to have lost the sharp puppy teeth and have some sense—a four- or five-month-old Dachshund can still be molded into a fine companion, not taking as much time as an eight- to twelve-week-old puppy but offering your old-timer some companionship.

I wouldn't do it if your senior is over twelve, but when she's nine or ten, the introduction should not be too traumatic. But, there are exceptions. When my year-old wire Miniature, Homer, left to go live with his six-year-old mother and Schnipful, who was over fifteen, there were no problems, and the "old man" adjusted marvelously well. The ironic part here was that Homer had been sold to Marie and Phil when he was barely six weeks old, but one of the reasons they left him with me was that they were concerned about the older dog and thought a young puppy would be too much. In the back of our minds was the reality that Schnipful would not be with them much longer! Homer, however, is a pensive, gentle dog, and the "old man" has perked up!

I sometimes wonder if my seniors live so long because my dogs are all house dogs and range in age from six-week-old litters, kept in the kitchen, to the matriarch or patriarch of the house. The youngsters keep life lively and interesting and coax the seniors into more outside time and even an occasional romp.

Give special care to a senior citizen.

You must never put your old-timer's nose out of joint, however, by cutting back on his time. If anything, give him more individual attention.

A younger dog can act as ears and eyes for a Dachshund losing his hearing or forming cataracts and even for one who is blind. They sense the needs of their not-so-spry companion and help as they can. (The Dachshund is such a delight to live with that most people always want another one as a companion for the one they have lived with for a year or so.) Older dogs often become insecure when noise or unfamiliar situations startle them. A pair of younger ears to sound an alarm reassures them.

You'll notice as your dog ages that you will be able to leave the room and even the house without disturbing her! You'll also be able to come into the house and find her still sleeping, snoring contentedly. It is a lonely feeling not to be greeted at the door, and perhaps to prepare for that, you may want to bring in another dog when your Dachshund is five or six. You'll have an age gap that will be comfortable, and you won't feel that the younger dog is a replacement for the one you lose because he's been there and has been his own "person" and will have his *own* name. (I feel strongly that you should not name your second dog after your first. This won't happen, of course, if your first Dachshund is still with you.)

Remember, old dogs can sometimes be crotchety and demanding, and they don't like changes in their routine, though they adapt. And they snore! But, they are also dignified and still very much the loving dog they always were—they just show it in different ways, and when you look into their eyes, clouded by time, they look back at you with such patience and such wisdom and such dignity. And so much love!

Make sure you have periodical checks of stool, urine and teeth so you can keep your oldster comfortable. See if your veterinarian recommends a senior diet or one specific to your dog's physical needs or problems.

Make sure she is warm where she sleeps and free from drafts, and make allowances for her fading eyesight and her not-too-keen hearing. At some point, she will no longer be pretending not to hear you.

I always leave a light on in the kitchen and make sure there is a spotlight on when they do go out in the dark. You should also be aware of how your oldster handles any stairs or steps and help him accordingly.

If you walk him, keep the pace moderate and cut the distance down gradually. Try to stop before he tires; remember, he also has to walk back to the house.

Feed smaller meals more often because sometimes they forget they ate and will drive you crazy!

I always cover their favorite sleeping place with a mattress pad that has a rubber side, and so, if they have an accident during the night or in the daytime when you're not there, it won't soil their bedding or the chair.

Saying Goodbye

The last thing you have to do is the hardest—knowing when to let go. Your heart won't like it, but your head has to rule here. Hopefully, all of them will die peacefully in their sleep, but we know that's not reality. Of all the dogs I have had, only my little Jen went that way. And she really didn't die in her sleep, since I had put her in her open crate while I dressed hurriedly to take her to my veterinarian. When I got back to her, she had slipped away. Should that happen to your Dachshund—that he slip away while you are not there or are asleep—simply gather him up wrapped in a blanket and take him to your veterinarian. Knowing ahead of time what to do with him makes it easier. I personally have never buried a dog. I plant a tree in his name. But that is *my* way.

And of all the ones I have lost, I have only requested the ashes of one, my soulmate, Bizzy. All of them have been special, but she was something more. I thought I would never be able to handle her death, but I have, and I am comfortable having her ashes in a container in the house. I am not sure what I will eventually do with them, but for now, where they are is fine.

Please remember that it's the *quality* of your Dachshund's life that's important, and when pain and lack of dignity take that quality away, we have to make a decision. If we don't, we're keeping them alive for us, and that is selfish. Remember them as light and sunshine, but when they become darkness, and suffering takes away their delight in life, it's time. I promise you, your head will know. Your veterinarian will not make the decision for you. You have to read between the lines of what he's telling you and keep your heart quiet while you make the best decision for your dog.

Full Circle

Your next Dachshund will be in so many ways the same but oh, so different—so very much his "own" person—because that's the way this breed is. But you know that already if you've lived with one! And he will make you laugh and shower you with love and want to spend his life being your best friend.

So, here's to new beginnings and bonds that will grow with the years and adventures galore as your new companion eases his way into your world. And then you will be back to where you started, and if it's been a long time, there are always Chapters 3 and 4 to refresh your memory. I'm also sure that you will find the following chapters interesting and informative, written by people who are competent in their respective fields and who will deal with things you need to know in areas I did not cover.

There are so many aspects of life open to you and your Dachshund that I am sure you are not aware of and may want to explore after you read the following sections. I hope I've given you a favorable impression of this breed—one I dearly love. Now you can move on to activities that will show you how adaptable and how intelligent this little hound can be. She is an ambassador of goodwill and friendship, bringing delight and laughter to so many places. And she'll love taking you along for the ride!

Have fun!

Your Happy, Healthy Pet

Your Dog's Name _____

Name on Your Dog's Pedigree (if your dog has one) _____

_____

Where Your Dog Came From _____

_____

Your Dog's Birthday _____

Your Dog's Veterinarian

    Name _____

    Address _____

    Phone Number _____

    Emergency Number _____

Your Dog's Health

    Vaccines

    type _____ date given _____

    type _____ date given _____

    type _____ date given _____

    type _____ date given _____

    Heartworm

    date tested _____ type used _____ start date _____

Your Dog's License Number _____

Groomer's Name and Number _____

Dogsitter/Walker's Name and Number _____

Awards Your Dog Has Won

    Award _____ date earned _____

    Award _____ date earned _____

part three

Enjoying

your

Dog

chapter 8

Basic
Training

by Ian Dunbar, Ph.D., MRCVS

Training is the jewel in the crown—the most important aspect of doggy husbandry. There is no more important variable influencing dog behavior and temperament than the dog's education: A well-trained, well-behaved and good-natured puppydog is always a joy to live with, but an untrained and uncivilized dog can be a perpetual nightmare. Moreover, deny the dog an education and it will not have the opportunity to fulfill its own canine potential; neither will it have the ability to communicate effectively with its human companions.

Luckily, modern psychological training methods are easy, efficient and effective and, above all, considerably dog-friendly and user-friendly. Doggy education is as simple as it is enjoyable. But before you can have a good time play-training with your new dog, you have to learn what to do and how to do it. There is no bigger variable influencing the success of dog training than the *owner's* experience and expertise. *Before you embark on the dog's education, you must first educate yourself.*

Basic Training for Owners

Ideally, basic owner training should begin well *before* you select your dog. Find out all you can about your chosen breed first, then master rudimentary training and handling skills. If you already have your puppy/dog, owner training is a dire emergency—the clock is running! Especially for puppies, the first few weeks at home are the most important and influential days in the dog's life. Indeed, the cause of most adolescent and adult problems may be traced back to the initial days the pup explores his new home. This is the time to establish the *status quo*—to teach the puppy/dog how you would like him to behave and so prevent otherwise quite predictable problems.

In addition to consulting breeders and breed books such as this one (which understandably have a positive breed bias), seek out as many pet owners with your breed you can find. Good points are obvious. What you want to find out are the breed-specific *problems*, so you can nip them in the bud. In particular, you should talk to owners with *adolescent* dogs and make a list of all anticipated problems. Most important, *test drive* at least half a dozen adolescent and adult dogs of your breed yourself. An eight-week-old puppy is deceptively easy to handle, but she will acquire adult size, speed and strength in just four months, so you should learn now what to prepare for.

Puppy and pet dog training classes offer a convenient venue to locate pet owners and observe dogs in action. For a list of suitable trainers in your area, contact the Association of Pet Dog Trainers (see Chapter 13). You may also begin your basic owner training by observing other owners in class. Watch as many classes and test drive as many dogs as possible. Select an upbeat, dog-friendly, people-friendly, fun-and-games, puppydog pet training class to learn the ropes. Also, watch training videos and read training books (see Chapter 12). You must find out what to do and how to do it *before* you have to do it.

Principles of Training

Most people think training comprises teaching the dog to do things such as sit, speak and roll over, but even a four-week-old pup knows how to do these things already. Instead, the first step in training involves teaching the dog human words for each dog behavior and activity and for each aspect of the dog's environment. That way you, the owner, can more easily participate in the dog's domestic education by directing him to perform specific actions appropriately, that is, at the right time, in the right place, and so on. Training opens communication channels, enabling an educated dog to at least understand the owner's requests.

In addition to teaching a dog *what* we want her to do, it is also necessary to teach her *why* she should do what we ask. Indeed, 95 percent of training revolves around motivating the dog *to want to do* what we want. Dogs often understand what their owners want; they just don't see the point of doing it—especially when the owner's repetitively boring and seemingly senseless instructions are totally at odds with much more pressing and exciting doggy distractions. It is not so much the dog who is being stubborn or dominant; rather, it is the owner who has failed to acknowledge the dog's needs and feelings and to approach training from the dog's point of view.

The Meaning of Instructions

The secret to successful training is learning how to use training lures to predict or prompt specific behaviors—to coax the dog to do what you want *when* you want. Any highly valued object (such as a treat or toy) may be used as a lure, which the dog will follow with his eyes and nose. Moving the lure in specific ways entices the dog to move his nose, head and entire body in specific ways. In fact, by learning the art of manipulating various lures, it is possible to teach the dog to assume virtually any body position and perform any action. Once you have control over the expression of the dog's behaviors and can elicit any body position or behavior at will, you can easily teach the dog to perform on request.

Tell your dog what you want him to do, use a lure to entice him to respond correctly, then profusely praise

Teach your dog words for each activity he needs to know, like down.

and maybe reward him once he performs the desired action. For example, verbally request "Fido, sit!" while you move a squeaky toy upwards and backwards over the dog's muzzle (lure-movement and hand signal), smile knowingly as he looks up (to follow the lure) and sits down (as a result of canine anatomical engineering), then praise him to distraction ("Gooood Fido!"). Squeak the toy, offer a training treat and give your dog and yourself a pat on the back.

Being able to elicit desired responses over and over enables the owner to reward the dog over and over. Consequently, the dog begins to think training is fun. For example, the more the dog is rewarded for sitting, the more she enjoys sitting. Eventually the dog comes to realize that, whereas most sitting is appreciated, sitting immediately upon request usually prompts especially enthusiastic praise and a slew of high-level rewards. The dog begins to sit on cue much of the time, showing that she is starting to grasp the meaning of the owner's verbal request and hand signal.

Why Comply?

Most dogs enjoy initial lure/reward training and are only too happy to comply with their owners' wishes. Unfortunately, repetitive drilling without appreciative feedback tends to diminish the dog's enthusiasm until he eventually fails to see the point of complying anymore. Moreover, as the dog approaches adolescence he becomes more easily distracted as he develops other interests. Lengthy sessions with repetitive exercises tend to bore and demotivate both parties. If it's not fun, the owner doesn't do it and neither does the dog.

Integrate training into your dog's life: The greater number of training sessions each day and the *shorter* they are, the more willingly compliant your dog will become. Make sure to have a short (just a few seconds) training interlude before every enjoyable canine activity. For example, ask your dog to sit to greet people, to sit before you throw his Frisbee, and to sit for his supper. Really, sitting is no different from a canine "please." Also, include numerous short training interludes during every enjoyable canine pastime, for example, when playing with the dog or when he is running in the park. In this fashion, doggy distractions may be effectively converted into rewards for training. Just as all games have rules, fun becomes training . . . and training becomes fun.

Eventually, rewards actually become unnecessary to continue motivating your dog. If trained with consideration and kindness, performing the desired behaviors will become self-rewarding and, in a sense, your dog will motivate himself. Just as it is not necessary to reward a human companion during an enjoyable walk in the park, or following a game of tennis, it is hardly necessary to reward our best friend—the dog—for walking by our side or while playing fetch. Human company during enjoyable activities is reward enough for most dogs.

Even though your dog has become self-motivating, it's still good to praise and pet him a lot and offer rewards once in a while, especially for a good job well done. And if for no other reason, praising and rewarding others is good for the human heart.

To train your dog, you need gentle hands, a loving heart and a good attitude.

Punishment

Without a doubt, lure/reward training is by far the best way to teach: Entice your dog to do what you want and then reward him for doing so. Unfortunately, a human shortcoming is to take the good for granted and to moan and groan at the bad. Specifically, the dog's many good behaviors are ignored while the owner focuses on punishing the dog for making mistakes. In extreme cases, instruction is *limited* to punishing mistakes made by a trainee dog, child, employee or husband, even though it has been proven punishment training is notoriously inefficient and ineffective and is decidedly unfriendly and combative. It teaches the dog that training is a drag, almost as quickly as it teaches the dog to dislike his trainer. Why treat our best friends like our worst enemies?

Punishment training is also much more laborious and time consuming. Whereas it takes only a finite amount of time to teach a dog what to chew, for example, it takes much, much longer to punish the dog for each and every mistake. Remember, *there is only one right way!* So why not teach that right way from the outset?!

103

To make matters worse, punishment training causes severe lapses in the dog's reliability. Since it is obviously impossible to punish the dog each and every time she misbehaves, the dog quickly learns to distinguish between those times when she must comply (so as to avoid impending punishment) and those times when she need not comply, because punishment is impossible. Such times include when the dog is off leash and only six feet away, when the owner is otherwise engaged (talking to a friend, watching television, taking a shower, tending to the baby or chatting on the telephone), or when the dog is left at home alone.

Instances of misbehavior will be numerous when the owner is away, because even when the dog complied in the owner's looming presence, he did so unwillingly. The dog was forced to act against his will, rather than moulding his will to want to please. Hence, when the owner is absent, not only does the dog know he need not comply, he simply does not want to. Again, the trainee is not a stubborn vindictive beast, but rather the trainer has failed to teach.

Punishment training invariably creates unpredictable Jekyll and Hyde behavior.

Trainer's Tools

Many training books extol the virtues of a vast array of training paraphernalia and electronic and metallic gizmos, most of which are designed for canine restraint, correction and punishment, rather than for actual facilitation of doggy education. In reality, most effective training tools are not found in stores; they come from within ourselves. In addition to a willing dog, all you really need is a functional human brain, gentle hands, a loving heart and a good attitude.

In terms of equipment, all dogs do require a quality buckle collar to sport dog tags and to attach the leash (for safety and to comply with local leash laws). Hollow chewtoys (like Kongs or sterilized longbones) and a dog bed or collapsible crate are a must for housetraining. Three additional tools are required:

1. specific lures (training treats and toys) to predict and prompt specific desired behaviors;

2. rewards (praise, affection, training treats and toys) to reinforce for the dog what a lot of fun it all is; and

3. knowledge—how to convert the dog's favorite activities and games (potential distractions to training) into "life-rewards," which may be employed to facilitate training.

The most powerful of these is *knowledge*. Education is the key! Watch training classes, participate in training classes, watch videos, read books, enjoy playtraining with your dog, and then your dog will say "Please," and your dog will say "Thank you!"

Housetraining

If dogs were left to their own devices, certainly they would chew, dig and bark for entertainment and then no doubt highlight a few areas of their living space with sprinkles of urine, in much the same way we decorate by hanging pictures. Consequently, when we ask a dog to live with us, we must teach him *where* he may dig and perform his toilet duties, *what* he may chew and *when* he may bark. After all, when left at home alone for many hours, we cannot expect the dog to amuse himself by completing crosswords or watching the soaps on TV!

Also, it would be decidedly unfair to keep the house rules a secret from the dog, and then get angry and punish the poor critter for inevitably transgressing rules he did not even know existed. Remember, without adequate education and guidance, the dog will be forced to establish his own rules—doggy rules—that most probably will be at odds with the owner's view of domestic living.

Since most problems develop during the first few days the dog is at home, prospective dog owners must be certain they are quite clear about the principles of housetraining *before* they get a dog. Early misbehaviors quickly become established as the status quo—

becoming firmly entrenched as hard-to-break bad habits, which set the precedent for years to come. Make sure to teach your dog good habits right from the start. Good habits are just as hard to break as bad ones!

Ideally, when a new dog comes home, try to arrange for someone to be present for as much as possible during the first few days (for adult dogs) or weeks for puppies. With only a little forethought, it is surprisingly easy to find a puppy sitter, such as a retired person, who would be willing to eat from your refrigerator and watch your television while keeping an eye on the newcomer to encourage the dog to play with chewtoys and to ensure he goes outside on a regular basis.

POTTY TRAINING

To teach the dog where to relieve himself:

1. never let him make a single mistake;
2. let him know where you want him to go; and
3. handsomely reward him for doing so: "GOOOOOOOD DOG!!!" liver treat, liver treat, liver treat!

PREVENTING MISTAKES

A single mistake is a training disaster, since it heralds many more in future weeks. And each time the dog soils the house, this further reinforces the dog's unfortunate preference for an indoor, carpeted toilet. *Do not let an unhousetrained dog have full run of the house if you are away from home or cannot pay full attention.* Instead, confine the dog to an area where elimination is appropriate, such as an outdoor run or, better still, a small, comfortable indoor kennel with access to an outdoor run. When confined in this manner, most dogs will naturally housetrain themselves.

If that's not possible, confine the dog to an area, such as a utility room, kitchen, basement or garage, where elimination may not be desired in the long run but as an interim measure it is certainly preferable to doing it all around the house. Use newspaper to cover the floor of the dog's day room. The newspaper may be used to soak up the urine and to wrap up and dispose of the feces. Once your dog develops a preferred spot for eliminating, it is only necessary to cover that part of the floor with newspaper. The smaller papered area may then be moved (only a little each day) towards the door to the outside. Thus the dog will develop the tendency to go to the door when he needs to relieve himself.

Never confine an unhousetrained dog to a crate for long periods. Doing so would force the dog to soil the crate and ruin its usefulness as an aid for housetraining (see the following discussion).

The first few weeks at home are the most important and influential in your dog's life.

TEACHING WHERE

In order to teach your dog where you would like her to do her business, you have to be there to direct the proceedings—an obvious, yet often neglected, fact of life. In order to be there to teach the dog *where* to go, you need to know *when* she needs to go. Indeed, the success of housetraining depends on the owner's ability to predict these times. Certainly, a regular feeding schedule will facilitate prediction somewhat, but there is nothing like "loading the deck" and influencing the timing of the outcome yourself!

Whenever you are at home, make sure the dog is under constant supervision and/or confined to a small area. If already well trained, simply instruct the dog to lie down in his bed or basket. Alternatively, confine the dog to a crate (doggy den) or tie-down (a short, 18-inch lead that can be clipped to an eye hook in the baseboard). Short-term close confinement strongly inhibits urination and defecation, since the dog does not want to soil his sleeping area. Thus, when you release the puppydog each hour, he will definitely need to urinate immediately and defecate every third or fourth hour. Keep the dog confined to his doggy den and take him to his intended toilet area each hour, every hour, and on the hour.

When taking your dog outside, instruct him to sit quietly before opening the door—he will soon learn to sit by the door when he needs to go out!

TEACHING WHY

Being able to predict when the dog needs to go enables the owner to be on the spot to praise and reward the dog. Each hour, hurry the dog to the intended toilet area in the yard, issue the appropriate instruction ("Go pee!" or "Go poop!"), then give the dog three to four minutes to produce. Praise and offer a couple of training treats when successful. The treats are important because many people fail to praise their dogs with feeling . . . and housetraining is hardly the time for understatement. So either loosen up and enthusiastically praise that dog: "Wuzzzer-wuzzer-wuzzer, hoooser good wuffer den? Hoooo went pee for Daddy?" Or say "Good dog!" as best you can and offer the treats for effect.

Following elimination is an ideal time for a spot of playtraining in the yard or house. Also, an empty dog may be allowed greater freedom around the house for the next half hour or so, just as long as you keep an eye out to make sure he does not get into other kinds of mischief. If you are preoccupied and cannot pay full attention, confine the dog to his doggy den once more to enjoy a peaceful snooze or to play with his many chewtoys.

If your dog does not eliminate within the allotted time outside—no biggie! Back to his doggy den, and then try again after another hour.

As I own large dogs, I always feel more relaxed walking an empty dog, knowing that I will not need to finish our stroll weighted down with bags of feces! Beware of falling into the trap of walking the dog to get it to eliminate. The good ol' dog walk is such an enormous highlight in the dog's life that it represents the single biggest potential reward in domestic dogdom. However, when in a hurry, or during inclement weather, many owners abruptly terminate the walk the moment the dog has done its business. This, in effect, severely punishes the dog for doing the right thing, in the right place at the right time. Consequently, many dogs become strongly inhibited from eliminating outdoors because they know it will signal an abrupt end to an otherwise thoroughly enjoyable walk.

Instead, instruct the dog to relieve himself in the yard prior to going for a walk. If you follow the above instructions, most dogs soon learn to eliminate on cue. As soon as the dog eliminates, praise (and offer a treat or two)—"Good dog! Let's go walkies!" Use the walk as a reward for eliminating in the yard. If the dog does not go, put him back in his doggy den and think about a walk later on. You will find with a "No feces–no walk" policy, your dog will become one of the fastest defecators in the business.

If you do not have a back yard, instruct the dog to eliminate right outside your front door prior to the walk. Not only will this facilitate clean up and disposal of the feces in your own trash can but, also, the walk may again be used as a colossal reward.

CHEWING AND BARKING

Short-term close confinement also teaches the dog that occasional quiet moments are a reality of domestic living. Your puppydog is extremely impressionable during his first few weeks at home. Regular

confinement at this time soon exerts a calming influ-
ence over the dog's personality. Remember, once the
dog is housetrained and calmer, there will be a whole
lifetime ahead for the dog to enjoy full run of the
house and garden. On the other hand, by letting the
newcomer have unrestricted access to the entire household and allowing him to run willy-nilly, he will most
certainly develop a bunch of behavior problems in
short order, no doubt necessitating confinement later
in life. It would not be fair to remedially restrain and
confine a dog you have trained, through neglect, to
run free.

When confining the dog, make sure he always has an
impressive array of suitable chewtoys. Kongs and sterilized longbones (both readily available from pet stores)
make the best chewtoys, since they are hollow and may
be stuffed with treats to heighten the dog's interest.
For example, by stuffing the little hole at the top of a
Kong with a small piece of freeze-dried liver, the dog
will not want to leave it alone.

Remember, treats do not have to be junk food and they
certainly should not represent extra calories. Rather,
treats should be part of each dog's regular daily diet:

*Make sure your
puppy has suit-
able chewtoys.*

Some food may be
served in the dog's
bowl for breakfast and
dinner, some food
may be used as train-
ing treats, and some
food may be used for
stuffing chewtoys. I
regularly stuff my
dogs' many Kongs
with different shaped
biscuits and kibble.
The kibble seems to fall out fairly easily, as do the
oval-shaped biscuits, thus rewarding the dog instanta-
neously for checking out the chewtoys. The bone-
shaped biscuits fall out after a while, rewarding the dog
for worrying at the chewtoy. But the triangular biscuits
never come out. They remain inside the Kong as lures,

maintaining the dog's fascination with its chewtoy. To further focus the dog's interest, I always make sure to flavor the triangular biscuits by rubbing them with a little cheese or freeze-dried liver.

If stuffed chewtoys are reserved especially for times the dog is confined, the puppydog will soon learn to enjoy quiet moments in her doggy den and she will quickly develop a chewtoy habit—a good habit! This is a simple *passive training* process; all the owner has to do is set up the situation and the dog all but trains herself—easy and effective. Even when the dog is given run of the house, her first inclination will be to indulge her rewarding chewtoy habit rather than destroying less-attractive household articles, such as curtains, carpets, chairs and compact disks. Similarly, a chewtoy chewer will be less inclined to scratch and chew herself excessively. Also, if the dog busies herself as a recreational chewer, she will be less inclined to develop into a recreational barker or digger when left at home alone.

Stuff a number of chewtoys whenever the dog is left confined and remove the extra-special-tasting treats when you return. Your dog will now amuse himself with his chewtoys before falling asleep and then resume playing with his chewtoys when he expects you to return. Since most owner-absent misbehavior happens right after you leave and right before your expected return, your puppydog will now be conveniently preoccupied with his chewtoys at these times.

Come and Sit

Most puppies will happily approach virtually anyone, whether called or not; that is, until they collide with

To teach come, call your dog, open your arms as a welcoming signal, wave a toy or a treat and praise for every step in your direction.

adolescence and develop other more important doggy interests, such as sniffing a multiplicity of exquisite odors on the grass. Your mission, Mr. and/or Ms. Owner, is to teach and reward the pup for coming reliably, willingly and happily when called—and you have just three months to get it done. Unless adequately reinforced, your puppy's tendency to approach people will self-destruct by adolescence.

Call your dog ("Fido, come!"), open your arms (and maybe squat down) as a welcoming signal, waggle a treat or toy as a lure, and reward the puppydog when he comes running. Do not wait to praise the dog until he reaches you—he may come 95 percent of the way and then run off after some distraction. Instead, praise the dog's *first* step towards you and continue praising enthusiastically for *every* step he takes in your direction.

When the rapidly approaching puppy dog is three lengths away from impact, instruct him to sit ("Fido, sit!") and hold the lure in front of you in an outstretched hand to prevent him from hitting you midchest and knocking you flat on your back! As Fido decelerates to nose the lure, move the treat upwards and backwards just over his muzzle with an upwards motion of your extended arm (palm-upwards). As the dog looks up to follow the lure, he will sit down (if he jumps up, you are holding the lure too high). Praise the dog for sitting. Move backwards and call him again. Repeat this many times over, always praising when Fido comes and sits; on occasion, reward him.

For the first couple of trials, use a training treat both as a lure to entice the dog to come and sit and as a reward for doing so. Thereafter, try to use different items as lures and rewards. For example, lure the dog with a Kong or Frisbee but reward her with a food treat. Or lure the dog with a food treat but pat her and throw a tennis ball as a reward. After just a few repetitions, dispense with the lures and rewards; the dog will begin to respond willingly to your verbal requests and hand signals just for the prospect of praise from your heart and affection from your hands.

Instruct every family member, friend and visitor how to get the dog to come and sit. Invite people over for a series of pooch parties; do not keep the pup a secret— let other people enjoy this puppy, and let the pup enjoy other people. Puppydog parties are not only fun, they easily attract a lot of people to help *you* train *your* dog. Unless you teach your dog *how* to meet people, that is, to sit for greetings, no doubt the dog will resort to jumping up. Then you and the visitors will get annoyed, and the dog will be punished. This is not fair. *Send out those invitations for puppy parties and teach your dog to be mannerly and socially acceptable.*

Even though your dog quickly masters obedient recalls in the house, his reliability may falter when playing in the back yard or local park. Ironically, it is *the owner* who has unintentionally trained the dog *not* to respond in these instances. By allowing the dog to play and run around and otherwise have a good time, but then to call the dog to put him on leash to take him home, the dog quickly learns playing is fun but training is a drag. Thus, playing in the park becomes a severe distraction, which works against training. Bad news!

Instead, whether playing with the dog off leash or on leash, request him to come at frequent intervals— say, every minute or so. On most occasions, praise and pet the dog for a few seconds while he is sitting, then tell him to go play again. For especially fast recalls, offer a couple of training treats and take the time to praise and pet the dog enthusiastically before releasing him. The dog will learn that coming when called is not necessarily the end of the play session, and neither is it the end of the world; rather, it signals an enjoyable, quality time-out with the owner before resuming play once more. In fact, playing in the park now becomes a very effective life-reward, which works to facilitate training by reinforcing each obedient and timely recall. Good news!

Sit, Down, Stand and Rollover

Teaching the dog a variety of body positions is easy for owner and dog, impressive for spectators and extremely useful for all. Using lure-reward techniques, it is possible to train several positions at once to verbal commands or hand signals (which impress the socks off onlookers).

Sit and **down**—the two control commands—prevent or resolve nearly a hundred behavior problems. For example, if the dog happily and obediently sits or lies down when requested, he cannot jump on visitors, dash out the front door, run around and chase its tail, pester other dogs, harass cats or annoy family, friends or strangers. Additionally, "sit" or "down" are better emergency commands for off-leash control.

It is easier to teach and maintain a reliable sit than maintain a reliable recall. *Sit* is the purest and simplest of commands—either the dog is sitting or he is not. If there is any change of circumstances or potential danger in the park, for example, simply instruct the dog to sit. If he sits, you have a number of options: allow the dog to resume playing when he is safe; walk up and put the dog on leash, or call the dog. The dog will be much more likely to come when called if he has already acknowledged his compliance by sitting. If the dog does not sit in the park—train him to!

Stand and **rollover-stay** are the two positions for examining the dog. Your veterinarian will love you to distraction if you take a little time to teach the dog to stand still and roll over and play possum. Also, your vet bills will be smaller. The rollover-stay is an especially useful command and is really just a variation of the down-stay: whereas the dog lies prone in the traditional down, she lies supine in the rollover-stay.

As with teaching come and sit, the training techniques to teach the dog to assume all other body positions on cue are user-friendly and dog-friendly. Simply give the appropriate request, lure the dog into the desired body position using a training treat or toy and then *praise* (and maybe reward) the dog as soon as he complies. Try not to touch the dog to get him to respond. If you teach the dog by guiding him into position, the dog will quickly learn that rump-pressure means sit, for example, but as yet you still have no control over your dog if he is just six feet away. It will still be necessary to teach the dog to sit on request. So do not make training a time-consuming two-step process; instead, teach the dog to sit to a verbal request or hand signal from the outset. Once the dog sits willingly when requested, by all means use your hands to pet the dog when he does so.

To teach *down* when the dog is already sitting, say "Fido, down!," hold the lure in one hand (palm down) and lower that hand to the floor between the dog's forepaws. As the dog lowers his head to follow the lure, slowly move the lure away from the dog just a fraction (in front of his paws). The dog will lie down as he stretches his nose forward to follow the lure. Praise the dog when he does so. If the dog stands up, you pulled the lure away too far and too quickly.

When teaching the dog to lie down from the standing position, say "down" and lower the lure to the floor as before. Once the dog has lowered his forequarters and assumed a play bow, gently and slowly move the lure *towards* the dog between his forelegs. Praise the dog as soon as his rear end plops down.

After just a couple of trials it will be possible to alternate sits and downs and have the dog energetically perform doggy push-ups. Praise the dog a lot, and after half a dozen or so push-ups reward the dog with a training treat or toy. You will notice the more energetically you move your arm—upwards (palm up) to get the dog to sit, and downwards (palm down) to get the dog to lie down—the more energetically the dog responds to your requests. Now try training the dog in silence and you will notice he has also learned to respond to hand signals. Yeah! Not too shabby for the first session.

To teach *stand* from the sitting position, say "Fido, stand," slowly move the lure half a dog-length away from the dog's nose, keeping it at nose level, and praise the dog as he stands to follow the lure. As soon

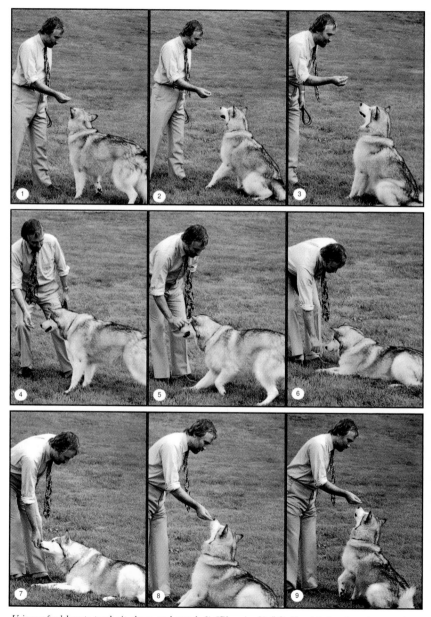

Using a food lure to teach sit, down and stand. 1) "Phoenix, Sit." 2) Hand palm upwards, move lure up and back over dog's muzzle. 3) "Good sit, Phoenix!" 4) "Phoenix, down." 5) Hand palm downwards, move lure down to lie between dog's forepaws. 6) "Phoenix, off. Good down, Phoenix!" 7) "Phoenix, sit!" 8) Palm upwards, move lure up and back, keeping it close to dog's muzzle. 9) "Good sit, Phoenix!"

10) "Phoenix, stand!" 11) Move lure away from dog at nose height, then lower it a tad. 12) "Phoenix, off! Good stand, Phoenix!" 13) "Phoenix, down!" 14) Hand palm downwards, move lure down to lie between dog's forepaws. 15) "Phoenix, off! Good down-stay, Phoenix!" 16) "Phoenix, stand!" 17) Move lure away from dog's muzzle up to nose height. 18) "Phoenix,off! Good stand-stay, Phoenix. Now we'll make the vet and groomer happy!"

as the dog stands, lower the lure to just beneath the
dog's chin to entice him to look down; otherwise he
will stand and then sit immediately. To prompt the dog
to stand from the down position, move the lure half a
dog-length upwards and away from the dog, holding
the lure at standing nose height from the floor.

Teaching *rollover* is best started from the down position, with the dog lying on one side, or at least with
both hind legs stretched out on the same side. Say
"Fido, bang!" and move the lure backwards and along-
side the dog's muzzle to its elbow (on the side of its
outstretched hind legs). Once the dog looks to the side
and backwards, very slowly move the lure upwards to
the dog's shoulder and backbone. Tickling the dog in
the goolies (groin area) often invokes a reflex-raising
of the hind leg as an appeasement gesture, which facilitates the tendency to roll over. If you move the lure
too quickly and the dog jumps into the standing position, have patience and start again. As soon as the dog
rolls onto its back, keep the lure stationary and mes-
merize the dog with a relaxing tummy rub.

To teach *rollover-stay* when the dog is standing or moving, say "Fido, bang!" and give the appropriate hand
signal (with index finger pointed and thumb cocked in
true Sam Spade fashion), then in one fluid movement
lure him to first lie down and then rollover-stay as above.

Teaching the dog to *stay* in each of the above four positions becomes a piece of cake after first teaching the
dog not to worry at the toy or treat training lure. This
is best accomplished by hand feeding dinner kibble.
Hold a piece of kibble firmly in your hand and softly
instruct "Off!" Ignore any licking and slobbering *for
however long the dog worries at the treat,* but say "Take it!"
and offer the kibble *the instant* the dog breaks contact
with his muzzle. Repeat this a few times, and then up
the ante and insist the dog remove his muzzle for one
whole second before offering the kibble. Then
progressively refine your criteria and have the dog
not touch your hand (or treat) for longer and longer
periods on each trial, such as for two seconds, four

seconds, then six, ten, fifteen, twenty, thirty seconds and so on. The dog soon learns: (1) worrying at the treat never gets results, whereas (2) noncontact is often rewarded after a variable time lapse.

Teaching *"Off!"* has many useful applications in its own right. Additionally, instructing the dog not to touch a training lure often produces spontaneous and magical stays. Request the dog to stand-stay, for example, and not to touch the lure. At first set your sights on a short two-second stay before rewarding the dog. (Remember, every long journey begins with a single step.) However, on subsequent trials, gradually and progressively increase the length of stay required to receive a reward. In no time at all your dog will stand calmly for a minute or so.

Relevancy Training

Once you have taught the dog what you expect her to do when requested to come, sit, lie down, stand, rollover and stay, the time is right to teach the dog *why* she should comply with your wishes. The secret is to have many (*many*) extremely short training interludes (two to five seconds each) at numerous (*numerous*) times during the course of the dog's day. Especially work with the dog immediately *before* the dog's good times and *during* the dog's good times. For example, ask your dog to sit and/or lie down each time before opening doors, serving meals, offering treats and tummy rubs; ask the dog to perform a few controlled doggy push-ups before letting her off-leash or throwing a tennis ball; and perhaps request the dog to sit-down-sit-stand-down-stand-rollover before inviting her to cuddle on the couch.

Similarly, request the dog to sit many times during play or on walks, and in no time at all the dog will be only too pleased to follow your instructions because he has learned that a compliant response heralds all sorts of goodies. Basically all you are trying to teach the dog is how to say please: "Please throw the tennis ball. Please may I snuggle on the couch."

119

Remember, whereas it is important to keep training interludes short, it is equally important to have many short sessions each and every day. The shortest (and most useful) session comprises asking the dog to sit and then go play during a play session. When trained this way, your dog will soon associate training with good times. In fact, the dog may be unable to distinguish between training and good times and, indeed, there should be no distinction. The warped concept that training involves forcing the dog to comply and/or dominating his will is totally at odds with the picture of a truly well-trained dog. In reality, enjoying a game of training with a dog is no different from enjoying a game of backgammon or tennis with a friend; and walking with a dog should be no different from strolling with buddies on the golf course.

Walk by Your Side

Many people attempt to teach a dog to heel by putting him on a leash and physically correcting the dog when he makes mistakes. There are a number of things seriously wrong with this approach, the first being that most people do not want precision heeling; rather, they simply want the dog to follow or walk by their side. Second, when physically restrained during "training," even though the dog may grudgingly mope by your side when "handcuffed" on leash, let's see what happens when he is off leash. History! The dog is in the next county because he never enjoyed walking with you on leash and you have no control over him off leash. So let's just teach the dog off leash from the outset to *want* to walk with us. Third, if the dog has not been trained to heel, it is a trifle hasty to think about punishing the poor dog for making mistakes and breaking heeling rules he didn't even know existed. This is simply not fair! Surely, if the dog had been adequately taught how to heel, he would seldom make mistakes and hence there would be no need to correct the dog. Remember, each mistake and each correction (punishment) advertise the trainer's inadequacy, not the dog's. The dog is not stubborn, he is not stupid and he is not bad. Even if he were, he would still require training, so let's train him properly.

Let's teach the dog to *enjoy* following us and to *want* to walk by our side offleash. Then it will be easier to teach high-precision off-leash heeling patterns if desired. After attaching the leash for safety on outdoor walks, but before going anywhere, it is necessary to teach the dog specifically not to pull. Now it will be much easier to teach on-leash walking and heeling because the dog already wants to walk with you, he is familiar with the desired walking and heeling positions and he knows not to pull.

FOLLOWING

Start by training your dog to follow you. Many puppies will follow if you simply walk away from them and maybe click your fingers or chuckle. Adult dogs may require additional enticement to stimulate them to follow, such as a training lure or, at the very least, a lively trainer. To teach the dog to follow: (1) keep walking and (2) walk away from the dog. If the dog attempts to lead or lag, change pace; slow down if the dog forges too far ahead, but speed up if he lags too far behind. Say "Steady!" or "Easy!" each time before you slow down and "Quickly!" or "Hustle!" each time before you speed up, and the dog will learn to change pace on cue. If the dog lags or leads too far, or if he wanders right or left, simply walk quickly in the opposite direction and maybe even run away from the dog and hide.

Practicing is a lot of fun; you can set up a course in your home, yard or park to do this. Indoors, entice the dog to follow upstairs, into a bedroom, into the bathroom, downstairs, around the living room couch, zigzagging between dining room chairs and into the kitchen for dinner. Outdoors, get the dog to follow around park benches, trees, shrubs and along walkways and lines in the grass. (For safety outdoors, it is advisable to attach a long line on the dog, but never exert corrective tension on the line.)

121

Remember, following has a lot to do with attitude—*your* attitude! Most probably your dog will *not* want to follow Mr. Grumpy Troll with the personality of wilted lettuce. Lighten up—walk with a jaunty step, whistle a happy tune, sing, skip and tell jokes to your dog and he will be right there by your side.

BY YOUR SIDE

It is smart to train the dog to walk close on one side or the other—either side will do, your choice. When walking, jogging or cycling, it is generally bad news to have the dog suddenly cut in front of you. In fact, I train my dogs to walk "By my side" and "Other side"—both very useful instructions. It is possible to position the dog fairly accurately by looking to the appropriate side and clicking your fingers or slapping your thigh on that side. A precise positioning may be attained by holding a training lure, such as a chewtoy, tennis ball, or food treat. Stop and stand still several times throughout the walk, just as you would when window shopping or meeting a friend. Use the lure to make sure the dog slows down and stays close whenever you stop.

When teaching the dog to heel, we generally want her to sit in heel position when we stop. Teach heel

Using a toy to teach sit-heel-sit sequences: 1) "Phoenix, heel!" Standing still, move lure up and back over dog's muzzle.... 2) To position dog sitting in heel position on your left side. 3) "Phoenix, heel!" wagging lure in left hand. Change lure to right hand in preparation for sit signal.

position at the standstill and the dog will learn that the default heel position is sitting by your side (left or right—your choice, unless you wish to compete in obedience trials, in which case the dog must heel on the left).

Several times a day, stand up and call your dog to come and sit in heel position—"Fido, heel!" For example, instruct the dog to come to heel each time there are commercials on TV, or each time you turn a page of a novel, and the dog will get it in a single evening.

Practice straight-line heeling and turns separately. With the dog sitting at heel, teach him to turn in place. After each quarter-turn, half-turn or full turn in place, lure the dog to sit at heel. Now it's time for short straight-line heeling sequences, no more than a few steps at a time. Always think of heeling in terms of Sit-Heel-Sit sequences—start and end with the dog in position and do your best to keep him there when moving. Progressively increase the number of steps in each sequence. When the dog remains close for 20 yards of straight-line heeling, it is time to add a few turns and then sign up for a happy-heeling obedience class to get some advice from the experts.

4) Use hand signal only to lure dog to sit as you stop. Eventually, dog will sit automatically at heel whenever you stop. 5) "Good dog!"

No Pulling on Leash

You can start teaching your dog not to pull on leash anywhere—in front of the television or outdoors—but regardless of location, you must not take a single step with tension in the leash. For a reason known only to dogs, even just a couple of paces of pulling on leash is intrinsically motivating and diabolically rewarding. Instead, attach the leash to the dog's collar, grasp the other end firmly with both hands held close to your chest, and stand still—do not budge an inch. Have somebody watch you with a stopwatch to time your progress, or else you will never believe this will work and so you will not even try the exercise, and your shoulder and the dog's neck will be traumatized for years to come.

Stand still and wait for the dog to stop pulling, and to sit and/or lie down. All dogs stop pulling and sit eventually. Most take only a couple of minutes; the all-time record is 22 ⅕ minutes. Time how long it takes. Gently praise the dog when he stops pulling, and as soon as he sits, enthusiastically praise the dog and take just one step forwards, then immediately stand still. This single step usually demonstrates the ballistic reinforcing nature of pulling on leash; most dogs explode to the end of the leash, so be prepared for the strain. Stand firm and wait for the dog to sit again. Repeat this half a dozen times and you will probably notice a progressive reduction in the force of the dog's one-step explosions and a radical reduction in the time it takes for the dog to sit each time.

As the dog learns "Sit we go" and "Pull we stop," she will begin to walk forward calmly with each single step and automatically sit when you stop. Now try two steps before you stop. Wooooooo! Scary! When the dog has mastered two steps at a time, try for three. After each success, progressively increase the number of steps in the sequence: try four steps and then six, eight, ten and twenty steps before stopping. Congratulations! You are now walking the dog on leash.

Whenever walking with the dog (off leash or on leash), make sure you stop periodically to practice a few position commands and stays before instructing the dog to "Walk on!" (Remember, you want the dog to be compliant everywhere, not just in the kitchen when his dinner is at hand.) For example, stopping every 25 yards to briefly train the dog amounts to over 200 training interludes within a single three-mile stroll. And each training session is in a different location. You will not believe the improvement within just the first mile of the first walk.

To put it another way, integrating training into a walk offers 200 separate opportunities to use the continuance of the walk as a reward to reinforce the dog's education. Moreover, some training interludes may comprise continuing education for the dog's walking skills: Alternate short periods of the dog walking calmly by your side with periods when the dog is allowed to sniff and investigate the environment. Now sniffing odors on the grass and meeting other dogs become rewards which reinforce the dog's calm and mannerly demeanor. Good Lord! Whatever next? Many enjoyable walks together of course. Happy trails!

THE IMPORTANCE OF TRICKS

Nothing will improve a dog's quality of life better than having a few tricks under its belt. Teaching any trick expands the dog's vocabulary, which facilitates communication and improves the owner's control. Also, specific tricks help prevent and resolve specific behavior problems. For example, by teaching the dog to fetch his toys, the dog learns carrying a toy makes the owner happy and, therefore, will be more likely to chew his toy than other inappropriate items.

More important, teaching tricks prompts owners to lighten up and train with a sunny disposition. Really, tricks should be no different from any other behaviors we put on cue. But they are. When teaching tricks, owners have a much sweeter attitude, which in turn motivates the dog and improves her willingness to comply. The dog feels tricks are a blast, but formal commands are a drag. In fact, tricks are so enjoyable, they may be used as rewards in training by asking the dog to come, sit and down-stay and then rollover for a tummy rub. Go on, try it: Crack a smile and even giggle when the dog promptly and willingly lies down and stays.

Most important, performing tricks prompts onlookers to smile and giggle. Many people are scared of dogs, especially large ones. And nothing can be more off-putting for a dog than to be constantly confronted by strangers who don't like him because of his size or the way he looks. Uneasy people put the dog on edge, causing him to back off and bark, only frightening people all the more. And so a vicious circle develops, with the people's fear fueling the dog's fear *and vice versa.* Instead, tie a pink ribbon to your dog's collar and practice all sorts of tricks on walks and in the park, and you will be pleasantly amazed how it changes people's attitudes toward your friendly dog. The dog's repertoire of tricks is limited only by the trainer's imagination. Below I have described three of my favorites:

SPEAK AND SHUSH

The training sequence involved in teaching a dog to bark on request is no different from that used when training any behavior on cue: request—lure—response—reward. As always, the secret of success lies in finding an effective lure. If the dog always barks at the doorbell, for example, say "Rover, speak!", have an accomplice ring the doorbell, then reward the dog for barking. After a few woofs, ask Rover to "Shush!", waggle a food treat under his nose (to entice him to sniff and thus to shush), praise him when quiet and eventually offer the treat as a reward. Alternate "Speak" and "Shush," progressively increasing the length of shush-time between each barking bout.

PLAYBOW

With the dog standing, say "Bow!" and lower the food lure (palm upwards) to rest between the dog's forepaws. Praise as the dog lowers her forequarters and sternum to the ground (as when teaching the down), but then lure the dog to stand and offer the treat. On successive trials, gradually increase the length of time the dog is required to remain in the playbow posture in order to gain a food reward. If the dog's rear end collapses into a down, say nothing and offer no reward; simply start over.

BE A BEAR

With the dog sitting backed into a corner to prevent him from toppling over backwards, say "Be a Bear!" With bent paw and palm down, raise a lure upwards and backwards along the top of the dog's muzzle. Praise the dog when he sits up on his haunches and offer the treat as a reward. To prevent the dog from standing on his hind legs, keep the lure closer to the dog's muzzle. On each trial, progressively increase the length of time the dog is required to sit up to receive a food reward. Since lure/reward training is so easy, teach the dog to stand and walk on his hind legs as well!

Teaching "Be a Bear"

chapter 9

Getting
Active
with your Dog

by Bardi McLennan

Once you and your dog have graduated from basic obedience training and are beginning to work together as a team, you can take part in the growing world of dog activities. There are so many fun things to do with your dog! Just remember, people and dogs don't always learn at the same pace, so don't be upset if you (or your dog) need more than two basic training courses before your team becomes operational. Even smart dogs don't go straight to college from kindergarten!

Just as there are events geared to certain types of dogs, so there are ones that are more appealing to certain types of people. In some

128

activities, you give the commands and your dog does the work (upland game hunting is one example), while in others, such as agility, you'll both get a workout. You may want to aim for prestigious titles to add to your dog's name, or you may want nothing more than the sheer enjoyment of being around other people and their dogs. Passive or active, participation has its own rewards.

Consider your dog's physical capabilities when looking into any of the canine activities. It's easy to see that a Basset Hound is not built for the racetrack, nor would a Chihuahua be the breed of choice for pulling a sled. A loyal dog will attempt almost anything you ask him to do, so it is up to you to know your dog's limitations. A dog must be physically sound in order to compete at any level in athletic activities, and being mentally sound is a definite plus. Advanced age, however, may not be a deterrent. Many dogs still hunt and herd at ten or twelve years of age. It's entirely possible for dogs to be "fit at 50." Take your dog for a checkup, explain to your vet the type of activity you have in mind and be guided by his or her findings.

All dogs seem to love playing flyball.

You needn't be restricted to breed-specific sports if it's only fun you're after. Certain AKC activities are limited to designated breeds; however, as each new trial, test or sport has grown in popularity, so has the variety of breeds encouraged to participate at a fun level.

But don't shortchange your fun, or that of your dog, by thinking only of the basic function of her breed. Once a dog has learned how to learn, she can be taught to do just about anything as long as the size of the dog is right for the job and you both think it is fun and rewarding. In other words, you are a team.

To get involved in any of the activities detailed in this chapter, look for the names and addresses of the organizations that sponsor them in Chapter 13. You can also ask your breeder or a local dog trainer for contacts.

You can compete in obedience trials with a well trained dog.

Official American Kennel Club Activities

The following tests and trials are some of the events sanctioned by the AKC and sponsored by various dog clubs. Your dog's expertise will be rewarded with impressive titles. You can participate just for fun, or be competitive and go for those awards.

OBEDIENCE

Training classes begin with pups as young as three months of age in kindergarten puppy training, then advance to pre-novice (all exercises on lead) and go on to novice, which is where you'll start off-lead work. In obedience classes dogs learn to sit, stay, heel and come through a variety of exercises. Once you've got the basics down, you can enter obedience trials and work toward earning your dog's first degree, a C.D. (Companion Dog).

The next level is called "Open," in which jumps and retrieves perk up the dog's interest. Passing grades in competition at this level earn a C.D.X. (Companion Dog Excellent). Beyond that lies the goal of the most ambitious—Utility (U.D. and even U.D.X. or OTCh, an Obedience Champion).

AGILITY

All dogs can participate in the latest canine sport to have gained worldwide popularity for its fun and excitement, agility. It began in England as a canine version of horse show-jumping, but because dogs are more agile and able to perform on verbal commands, extra feats were added such as climbing, balancing and racing through tunnels or in and out of weave poles.

Many of the obstacles (regulation or homemade) can be set up in your own backyard. If the agility bug bites, you could end up in international competition!

For starters, your dog should be obedience trained, even though, in the beginning, the lessons may all be taught on lead. Once the dog understands the commands (and you do, too), it's as easy as guiding the dog over a prescribed course, one obstacle at a time. In competition, the race is against the clock, so wear your running shoes! The dog starts with 200 points and the judge deducts for infractions and misadventures along the way.

All dogs seem to love agility and respond to it as if they were being turned loose in a playground paradise. Your dog's enthusiasm will be contagious; agility turns into great fun for dog and owner.

FIELD TRIALS AND HUNTING TESTS

There are field trials and hunting tests for the sporting breeds—retrievers, spaniels and pointing breeds, and for some hounds—Bassets, Beagles and Dachshunds. Field trials are competitive events that test a dog's ability to perform the functions for which she was bred. Hunting tests, which are open to retrievers,

---

TITLES AWARDED BY THE AKC

Conformation: Ch. (Champion)

Obedience: CD (Companion Dog); CDX (Companion Dog Excellent); UD (Utility Dog); UDX (Utility Dog Excellent); OTCh. (Obedience Trial Champion)

Field: JH (Junior Hunter); SH (Senior Hunter); MH (Master Hunter); AFCh. (Amateur Field Champion); FCh. (Field Champion)

Lure Coursing: JC (Junior Courser); SC (Senior Courser)

Herding: HT (Herding Tested); PT (Pre-Trial Tested); HS (Herding Started); HI (Herding Intermediate); HX (Herding Excellent); HCh. (Herding Champion)

Tracking: TD (Tracking Dog); TDX (Tracking Dog Excellent)

Agility: NAD (Novice Agility); OAD (Open Agility); ADX (Agility Excellent); MAX (Master Agility)

Earthdog Tests: JE (Junior Earthdog); SE (Senior Earthdog); ME (Master Earthdog)

Canine Good Citizen: CGC

Combination: DC (Dual Champion—Ch. and Fch.); TC (Triple Champion—Ch., Fch., and OTCh.)

spaniels and pointing breeds only, are noncompetitive
and are a means of judging the dog's ability as well as
that of the handler.

Hunting is a very large and complex part of canine
sports, and if you own one of the breeds that hunts, the
events are a great treat for your dog and you. He gets
to do what he was bred for, and you get to work with
him and watch him do it. You'll be proud of and
amazed at what your dog can do.

Fortunately, the AKC publishes a series of booklets on
these events, which outline the rules and regulations
and include a glossary of the sometimes complicated
terms. The AKC also publishes newsletters for field tri-
alers and hunting test enthusiasts. The United Kennel
Club (UKC) also has informative materials for the
hunter and his dog.

*Retrievers and
other sporting
breeds get to do
what they're
bred to in hunt-
ing tests.*

HERDING TESTS AND TRIALS

Herding, like hunting, dates
back to the first known uses man
made of dogs. The interest in
herding today is widespread,
and if you own a herding breed,
you can join in the activity.
Herding dogs are tested for
their natural skills to keep a
flock of ducks, sheep or cattle
together. If your dog shows
potential, you can start at the
testing level, where your dog can
earn a title for showing an inherent herding ability.
With training you can advance to the trial level, where
your dog should be capable of controlling even difficult livestock in diverse situations.

LURE COURSING

The AKC Tests and Trials for Lure Coursing are open
to traditional sighthounds—Greyhounds, Whippets,

Borzoi, Salukis, Afghan Hounds, Ibizan Hounds and Scottish Deerhounds—as well as to Basenjis and Rhodesian Ridgebacks. Hounds are judged on overall ability, follow, speed, agility and endurance. This is possibly the most exciting of the trials for spectators, because the speed and agility of the dogs is awesome to watch as they chase the lure (or "course") in heats of two or three dogs at a time.

TRACKING

Tracking is another activity in which almost any dog can compete because every dog that sniffs the ground when taken outdoors is, in fact, tracking. The hard part comes when the rules as to what, when and where the dog tracks are determined by a person, not the dog! Tracking tests cover a large area of fields, woods and roads. The tracks are laid hours before the dogs go to work on them, and include "tricks" like cross-tracks and sharp turns. If you're interested in search-and-rescue work, this is the place to start.

This tracking dog is hot on the trail.

EARTHDOG TESTS FOR SMALL TERRIERS AND DACHSHUNDS

These tests are open to Australian, Bedlington, Border, Cairn, Dandie Dinmont, Smooth and Wire Fox, Lakeland, Norfolk, Norwich, Scottish, Sealyham, Skye, Welsh and West Highland White Terriers as well as Dachshunds. The dogs need no prior training for this terrier sport. There is a qualifying test on the day of the event, so dog and handler learn the rules on the spot. These tests, or "digs," sometimes end with informal races in the late afternoon.

133

Here are some of the extracurricular obedience and
racing activities that are not regulated by the AKC or
UKC, but are generally run by clubs or a group of dog
fanciers and are often open to all.

Canine Freestyle This activity is something new on
the scene and is variously likened to dancing, dressage
or ice skating. It is meant to show the athleticism of the
dog, but also requires showmanship on the part of the
dog's handler. If you and your dog like to ham it up for
friends, you might want to look into freestyle.

*Lure coursing
lets sighthounds
do what they do
best—run!*

Scent Hurdle Racing Scent hurdle racing is purely a
fun activity sponsored by obedience clubs with members forming competing teams. The height of the hurdles is based on the size of the shortest dog on the
team. On a signal, one team dog is released on each of
two side-by-side courses and must clear every hurdle
before picking up its own dumbbell from a platform
and returning over the jumps to the handler. As each
dog returns, the next on that team is sent. Of course,
that is what the dogs are supposed to do. When the
dogs improvise (going under or around the hurdles,
stealing another dog's dumbbell, and so forth), it no
doubt frustrates the handlers, but just adds to the fun
for everyone else.

Flyball This type of racing is similar, but after negoti-
ating the four hurdles, the dog comes to a flyball box,
steps on a lever that releases a tennis ball into the air,

catches the ball and returns over the hurdles to the starting point. This game also becomes extremely fun for spectators because the dogs sometimes cheat by catching a ball released by the dog in the next lane. Three titles can be earned—Flyball Dog (F.D.), Flyball Dog Excellent (F.D.X.) and Flyball Dog Champion (Fb.D.Ch.)—all awarded by the North American Flyball Association, Inc.

Dogsledding The name conjures up the Rocky Mountains or the frigid North, but you can find dogsled clubs in such unlikely spots as Maryland, North Carolina and Virginia! Dogsledding is primarily for the Nordic breeds such as the Alaskan Malamutes, Siberian Huskies and Samoyeds, but other breeds can try. There are some practical backyard applications to this sport, too. With parental supervision, almost any strong dog could pull a child's sled.

Coming over the A-frame on an agility course.

These are just some of the many recreational ways you can get to know and understand your multifaceted dog better and have fun doing it.

chapter 10

Your Dog
and your
Family

by Bardi McLennan

Adding a dog automatically increases your family by one, no matter whether you live alone in an apartment or are part of a mother, father and six kids household. The single-person family is fair game for numerous and varied canine misconceptions as to who is dog and who pays the bills, whereas a dog in a houseful of children will consider himself to be just one of the gang, littermates all. One dog and one child may give a dog reason to believe they are both kids or both dogs.

Either interpretation requires parental supervision and sometimes speedy intervention.

As soon as one paw goes through the door into your home, Rufus (or Rufina) has to make many adjustments to become a part of your family. Your job is to make him fit in as painlessly as possible. An older dog may have some frame of reference from past experience, but to a 10-week-old puppy, everything is brand new: people, furniture, stairs, when and where people eat, sleep or watch TV, his own place and everyone else's space, smells, sounds, outdoors—everything!

Puppies, and newly acquired dogs of any age, do not need what we think of as "freedom." If you leave a new dog or puppy loose in the house, you will almost certainly return to chaotic destruction and the dog will forever after equate your homecoming with a time of punishment to be dreaded. It is unfair to give your dog what amounts to "freedom to get into trouble." Instead, confine him to a crate for brief periods of your absence (up to three or four hours) and, for the long haul, a workday for example, confine him to one untrashable area with his own toys, a bowl of water and a radio left on (low) in another room.

Lots of pets get along with each other just fine.

For the first few days, when not confined, put Rufus on a long leash tied to your wrist or waist. This umbilical cord method enables the dog to learn all about you from your body language and voice, and to learn by his own actions which things in the house are NO! and which ones are rewarded by "Good dog." House-training will be easier with the pup always by your side. Speaking of which, accidents do happen. That goal of "completely housetrained" takes up to a year, or the length of time it takes the pup to mature.

The All-Adult Family

Most dogs in an adults-only household today are likely to be latchkey pets, with no one home all day but the dog. When you return after a tough day on the job, the dog can and should be your relaxation therapy. But going home can instead be a daily frustration.

Separation anxiety is a very common problem for the dog in a working household. It may begin with whines and barks of loneliness, but it will soon escalate into a frenzied destruction derby. That is why it is so important to set aside the time to teach a dog to relax when left alone in his confined area and to understand that he can trust you to return.

Let the dog get used to your work schedule in easy stages. Confine him to one room and go in and out of that room over and over again. Be casual about it. No physical, voice or eye contact. When the pup no longer even notices your comings and goings, leave the house for varying lengths of time, returning to stay home for a few minutes and gradually increasing the time away. This training can take days, but the dog is learning that you haven't left him forever and that he can trust you.

Any time you leave the dog, but especially during this training period, be casual about your departure. No anxiety-building fond farewells. Just "Bye" and go! Remember the "Good dog" when you return to find everything more or less as you left it.

If things are a mess (or even a disaster) when you return, greet the dog, take him outside to eliminate, and then put him in his crate while you clean up. Rant and rave in the shower! *Do not* punish the dog. You were not there when it happened, and the rule is: Only punish as you catch the dog in the act of wrongdoing. Obviously, it makes sense to get your latchkey puppy when you'll have a week or two to spend on these training essentials.

Family weekend activities should include Rufus whenever possible. Depending on the pup's age, now is the time for a long walk in the park, playtime in the backyard, a hike in the woods. Socializing is as important as health care, good food and physical exercise, so visiting Aunt Emma or Uncle Harry and the next-door neighbor's dog or cat is essential to developing an out-going, friendly temperament in your pet.

If you are a single adult, socializing Rufus at home and away will prevent him from becoming overly protective of you (or just overly attached) and will also prevent such behavioral problems as dominance or fear of strangers.

Babies

Whether already here or on the way, babies figure larger than life in the eyes of a dog. If the dog is there first, let him in on all your baby preparations in the house. When baby arrives, let Rufus sniff any item of clothing that has been on the baby before Junior comes home. Then let Mom greet the dog first before introducing the new family member. Hold the baby down for the dog to see and sniff, but make sure some-one's holding the dog on lead in case of any sudden moves. Don't play keep-away or tease the dog with the baby, which only invites undesirable jump-ing up.

The dog and the baby are "family," and for starters can be treated almost as equals. Things rapidly change, however, espe-cially when baby takes to creeping around on all fours on the dog's turf or, better yet, has yummy pudding all over her face and hands! That's when a lot of things in the dog's and baby's lives become more separate than equal.

Dogs are perfect confidants.

Toddlers make terrible dog owners, but if you can't avoid the combination, use patient discipline (that is, positive teaching rather than punishment), and use time-outs before you run out of patience.

A dog and a baby (or toddler, or an assertive young child) should never be left alone together. Take the dog with you or confine him. With a baby or youngsters in the house, you'll have plenty of use for that wonderful canine safety device called a crate!

Young Children

Any dog in a house with kids will behave pretty much as the kids do, good or bad. But even good dogs and good children can get into trouble when play becomes rowdy and active.

Teach children how to play nicely with a puppy.

Legs bobbing up and down, shrill voices screeching, a ball hurtling overhead, all add up to exuberant frustration for a dog who's just trying to be part of the gang. In a pack of puppies, any legs or toys being chased would be caught by a set of teeth, and all the pups involved would understand that is how the game is played. Kids do not understand this, nor do parents tolerate it. Bring Rufus indoors before you have reason to regret it. This is time-out, not a punishment.

You can explain the situation to the children and tell them they must play quieter games until the puppy learns not to grab them with his mouth. Unfortunately, you can't explain it that easily to the dog. With adult supervision, they will learn how to play together.

Young children love to tease. Sticking their faces or wiggling their hands or fingers in the dog's face is teasing. To another person it might be just annoying, but it is threatening to a dog. There's another difference: We can make the child stop by an explanation, but the only way a dog can stop it is with a warning growl and then with teeth. Teasing is the major cause of children being bitten by their pets. Treat it seriously.

Older Children

The best age for a child to get a first dog is between the ages of 8 and 12. That's when kids are able to accept some real responsibility for their pet. Even so, take the child's vow of "I will never *ever* forget to feed (brush, walk, etc.) the dog" for what it's worth: a child's good intention at that moment. Most kids today have extra lessons, soccer practice, Little League, ballet, and so forth piled on top of school schedules. There will be many times when Mom will have to come to the dog's rescue. "I walked the dog for you so you can set the table for me" is one way to get around a missed appointment without laying on blame or guilt.

Kids in this age group make excellent obedience trainers because they are into the teaching/learning process themselves and they lack the self-consciousness of adults. Attending a dog show is something the whole family can enjoy, and watching Junior Showmanship may catch the eye of the kids. Older children can begin to get involved in many of the recreational activities that were reviewed in the previous chapter. Some of the agility obstacles, for example, can be set up in the backyard as a family project (with an adult making sure all the equipment is safe and secure for the dog).

Older kids are also beginning to look to the future, and may envision themselves as veterinarians or trainers or show dog handlers or writers of the next Lassie best-seller. Dogs are perfect confidants for these dreams. They won't tell a soul.

Other Pets

Introduce all pets tactfully. In a dog/cat situation, hold the dog, not the cat. Let two dogs meet on neutral turf—a stroll in the park or a walk down the street—with both on loose leads to permit all the normal canine ways of saying hello, including routine sniffing, circling, more sniffing, and so on. Small creatures such as hamsters, chinchillas or mice must be kept safe from their natural predators (dogs and cats).

Festive Family Occasions

Parties are great for people, but not necessarily for puppies. Until all the guests have arrived, put the dog in his crate or in a room where he won't be disturbed. A socialized dog can join the fun later as long as he's not underfoot, annoying guests or into the hors d'oeuvres.

There are a few dangers to consider, too. Doors opening and closing can allow a puppy to slip out unnoticed in the confusion, and you'll be organizing a search party instead of playing host or hostess. Party food and buffet service are not for dogs. Let Rufus party in his crate with a nice big dog biscuit.

At Christmas time, not only are tree decorations dangerous and breakable (and perhaps family heirlooms), but extreme caution should be taken with the lights, cords and outlets for the tree lights and any other festive lighting. Occasionally a dog lifts a leg, ignoring the fact that the tree is indoors. To avoid this, use a canine repellent, made for gardens, on the tree. Or keep him out of the tree room unless supervised. And whatever you do, *don't* invite trouble by hanging his toys on the tree!

Car Travel

Before you plan a vacation by car or RV with Rufus, be sure he enjoys car travel. Nothing spoils a holiday quicker than a carsick dog! Work within the dog's comfort level. Get in the car with the dog in his crate or attached to a canine car safety belt and just sit there until he relaxes. That's all. Next time, get in the car, turn on the engine and go nowhere. Just sit. When that is okay, turn on the engine and go around the block. Now you can go for a ride and include a stop where you get out, leaving the dog for a minute or two.

On a warm day, always park in the shade and leave windows open several inches. And return quickly. It only takes 10 minutes for a car to become an overheated steel death trap.

Motel or Pet Motel?

Not all motels or hotels accept pets, but you have a much better choice today than even a few years ago. To find a dog-friendly lodging, look at *On the Road Again With Man's Best Friend*, a series of directories that detail bed and breakfasts, inns, family resorts and other hotels/motels. Some places require a refundable deposit to cover any damage incurred by the dog. More B&Bs accept pets now, but some restrict the size.

If taking Rufus with you is not feasible, check out boarding kennels in your area. Your veterinarian may offer this service, or recommend a kennel or two he or she is familiar with. Go see the facilities for yourself, ask about exercise, diet, housing, and so on. Or, if you'd rather have Rufus stay home, look into bonded petsitters, many of whom will also bring in the mail and water your plants.

chapter 11

Your Dog
and your
Community

by Bardi McLennan

Step outside your home with your dog and you are no longer just family, you are both part of your community. This is when the phrase "responsible pet ownership" takes on serious implications. For starters, it means you pick up after your dog—not just occasionally, but every time your dog eliminates away from home. That means you have joined the Plastic Baggy Brigade! You always have plastic sandwich bags in your pocket and several in the car. It means you teach your kids how to use them, too. If you think this is "yucky," just imagine what

the person (a non-doggy person) who inadvertently steps in the mess thinks!

Your responsibility extends to your neighbors: To their ears (no annoying barking); to their property (their garbage, their lawn, their flower beds, their cat— especially their cat); to their kids (on bikes, at play); to their kids' toys and sports equipment.

There are numerous dog-related laws, ranging from simple dog licensing and leash laws to those holding you liable for any physical injury or property damage done by your dog. These laws are in place to protect everyone in the community, including you and your dog. There are town ordinances and state laws which are by no means the same in all towns or all states. Ignorance of the law won't get you off the hook. The time to find out what the laws are where you live is now.

Be sure your dog's license is current. This is not just a good local ordinance, it can make the difference between finding your lost dog or not.

Dressing your dog up makes him appealing to strangers.

Many states now require proof of rabies vaccination and that the dog has been spayed or neutered before issuing a license. At the same time, keep up the dog's annual immunizations.

Never let your dog run loose in the neighborhood. This will not only keep you on the right side of the leash law, it's the outdoor version of the rule about not giving your dog "freedom to get into trouble."

Good Canine Citizen

Sometimes it's hard for a dog's owner to assess whether or not the dog is sufficiently socialized to be accepted by the community at large. Does Rufus or Rufina display good, controlled behavior in public? The AKC's Canine Good Citizen program is available through many dog organizations. If your dog passes the test, the title "CGC" is earned.

The overall purpose is to turn your dog into a good neighbor and to teach you about your responsibility to your community as a dog owner. Here are the ten things your dog must do willingly:

1. Allow a stranger to handle him or her as a groomer or veterinarian would.
2. Accept a stranger stopping to chat with you.
3. Walk nicely on a loose lead.
4. Walk calmly through a crowd.
5. Sit and be petted by a stranger.
6. Sit and down on command.
7. Stay put when you move away.
8. Casually greet another dog.
9. React confidently to distractions.
10. Accept being tied up in a strange place and left alone for a few minutes.

Schools and Dogs

Schools are getting involved with pet ownership on an educational level. It has been proven that children who are kind to animals are humane in their attitude toward other people as adults.

A dog is a child's best friend, and so children are often primary pet owners, if not the primary caregivers. Unfortunately, they are also the ones most often bitten by dogs. This occurs due to a lack of understanding that pets, no matter how sweet, cuddly and loving, are still animals. Schools, along with parents, dog clubs, dog fanciers and the AKC, are working to change all that with video programs for children not only in grade school, but in the nursery school and pre-kindergarten age group. Teaching youngsters how to be responsible dog owners is important community work. When your dog has a CGC, volunteer to take part in an educational classroom event put on by your dog club.

Boy Scout Merit Badge

A Merit Badge for Dog Care can be earned by any Boy Scout ages 11 to 18. The requirements are not easy, but amount to a complete course in responsible dog care and general ownership. Here are just a few of the things a Scout must do to earn that badge:

Point out ten parts of the dog using the correct names.

Give a report (signed by parent or guardian) on your care of the dog (feeding, food used, housing, exercising, grooming and bathing), plus what has been done to keep the dog healthy.

Explain the right way to obedience train a dog, and demonstrate three comments.

Several of the requirements have to do with health care, including first aid, handling a hurt dog, and the dangers of home treatment for a serious ailment.

The final requirement is to know the local laws and ordinances involving dogs.

There are similar programs for Girl Scouts and 4-H members.

Local Clubs

Local dog clubs are no longer in existence just to put on a yearly dog show. Today, they are apt to be the hub of the community's involvement with pets. Dog clubs conduct educational forums with big-name speakers, stage demonstrations of canine talent in a busy mall and take dogs of various breeds to schools for classroom discussion.

The quickest way to feel accepted as a member in a club is to volunteer your services! Offer to help with something—anything—and watch your popularity (and your interest) grow.

Therapy Dogs

Once your dog has earned that essential CGC and reliably demonstrates a steady, calm temperament, you could look into what therapy dogs are doing in your area.

Therapy dogs go with their owners to visit patients at hospitals or nursing homes, generally remaining on leash but able to coax a pat from a stiffened hand, a smile from a blank face, a few words from sealed lips or a hug from someone in need of love.

Nursing homes cover a wide range of patient care. Some specialize in care of the elderly, some in the treatment of specific illnesses, some in physical therapy. Children's facilities also welcome visits from trained therapy dogs for boosting morale in their pediatric patients. Hospice care for the terminally ill and the at-home care of AIDS patients are other areas where this canine visiting is desperately needed. Therapy dog training comes first.

Your dog can make a difference in lots of lives.

There is a lot more involved than just taking your nice friendly pooch to someone's bedside. Doing therapy dog work involves your own emotional stability as well as that of your dog. But once you have met all the requirements for this work, making the rounds once a week or once a month with your therapy dog is possibly the most rewarding of all community activities.

Disaster Aid

This community service is definitely not for everyone, partly because it is time-consuming. The initial training is rigorous, and there can be no let-up in the continuing workouts, because members are on call 24 hours a day to go wherever they are needed at a moment's notice. But if you think you would like to be able to assist in a disaster, look into search-and-rescue work. The network of search-and-rescue volunteers is worldwide, and all members of the American Rescue Dog Association (ARDA) who are qualified to do this work are volunteers who train and maintain their own dogs.

Physical Aid

Most people are familiar with Seeing Eye dogs, which serve as blind people's eyes, but not with all the other work that dogs are trained to do to assist the disabled. Dogs are also specially trained to pull wheelchairs, carry school books, pick up dropped objects, open and close doors. Some also are ears for the deaf. All these assistance-trained dogs, by the way, are allowed anywhere "No Pet" signs exist (as are therapy dogs when properly identified). Getting started in any of this fascinating work requires a background in dog training and canine behavior, but there are also volunteer jobs ranging from answering the phone to cleaning out kennels to providing a foster home for a puppy. You have only to ask.

Making the rounds with your therapy dog can be very rewarding.

part four

Beyond
the
Basics

chapter 12

Recommended Reading

Books

ABOUT HEALTH CARE

Ackerman, Lowell. *Guide to Skin and Haircoat Problems in Dogs.* Loveland, Colo.: Alpine Publications, 1994.

Alderton, David. *The Dog Care Manual.* Hauppauge, N.Y.: Barron's Educational Series, Inc., 1986.

American Kennel Club. *American Kennel Club Dog Care and Training.* New York: Howell Book House, 1991.

Bamberger, Michelle, DVM. *Help! The Quick Guide to First Aid for Your Dog.* New York: Howell Book House, 1995.

Carlson, Delbert, DVM, and James Giffin, MD. *Dog Owner's Home Veterinary Handbook.* New York: Howell Book House, 1992.

DeBitetto, James, DVM, and Sarah Hodgson. *You & Your Puppy.* New York: Howell Book House, 1995.

Humphries, Jim, DVM. *Dr. Jim's Animal Clinic for Dogs.* New York: Howell Book House, 1994.

McGinnis, Terri. *The Well Dog Book.* New York: Random House, 1991.

Pitcairn, Richard and Susan. *Natural Health for Dogs.* Emmaus, Pa.: Rodale Press, 1982.

ABOUT DOG SHOWS

Hall, Lynn. *Dog Showing for Beginners.* New York: Howell Book House, 1994.

Nichols, Virginia Tuck. *How to Show Your Own Dog.* Neptune, N. J.: TFH, 1970.

Vanacore, Connie. *Dog Showing, An Owner's Guide.* New York: Howell Book House, 1990.

ABOUT TRAINING

Ammen, Amy. *Training in No Time*. New York: Howell Book House, 1995.

Baer, Ted. *Communicating With Your Dog*. Hauppauge, N.Y.: Barron's Educational Series, Inc., 1989.

Benjamin, Carol Lea. *Dog Problems*. New York: Howell Book House, 1989.

Benjamin, Carol Lea. *Dog Training for Kids*. New York: Howell Book House, 1988.

Benjamin, Carol Lea. *Mother Knows Best*. New York: Howell Book House, 1985.

Benjamin, Carol Lea. *Surviving Your Dog's Adolescence*. New York: Howell Book House, 1993.

Bohnenkamp, Gwen. *Manners for the Modern Dog*. San Francisco: Perfect Paws, 1990.

Dibra, Bashkim. *Dog Training by Bash*. New York: Dell, 1992.

Dunbar, Ian, PhD, MRCVS. *Dr. Dunbar's Good Little Dog Book*, James & Kenneth Publishers, 2140 Shattuck Ave. #2406, Berkeley, Calif. 94704. (510) 658–8588. Order from the publisher.

Dunbar, Ian, PhD, MRCVS. *How to Teach a New Dog Old Tricks*, James & Kenneth Publishers. Order from the publisher; address above.

Dunbar, Ian, PhD, MRCVS, and Gwen Bohnenkamp. Booklets on *Preventing Aggression; Housetraining; Chewing; Digging; Barking; Socialization; Fearfulness; and Fighting*, James & Kenneth Publishers. Order from the publisher; address above.

Evans, Job Michael. *People, Pooches and Problems*. New York: Howell Book House, 1991.

Kilcommons, Brian and Sarah Wilson. *Good Owners, Great Dogs*. New York: Warner Books, 1992.

McMains, Joel M. *Dog Logic—Companion Obedience*. New York: Howell Book House, 1992.

Rutherford, Clarice and David H. Neil, MRCVS. *How to Raise a Puppy You Can Live With*. Loveland, Colo.: Alpine Publications, 1982.

Volhard, Jack and Melissa Bartlett. *What All Good Dogs Should Know: The Sensible Way to Train*. New York: Howell Book House, 1991.

ABOUT BREEDING

Harris, Beth J. Finder. *Breeding a Litter, The Complete Book of Prenatal and Postnatal Care*. New York: Howell Book House, 1983.

Holst, Phyllis, DVM. *Canine Reproduction*. Loveland, Colo.: Alpine Publications, 1985.

Walkowicz, Chris and Bonnie Wilcox, DVM. *Successful Dog Breeding, The Complete Handbook of Canine Midwifery*. New York: Howell Book House, 1994.

About Activities

American Rescue Dog Association. *Search and Rescue Dogs*. New York: Howell Book House, 1991.

Barwig, Susan and Stewart Hilliard. *Schutzhund*. New York: Howell Book House, 1991.

Beaman, Arthur S. *Lure Coursing*. New York: Howell Book House, 1994.

Daniels, Julie. *Enjoying Dog Agility—From Backyard to Competition*. New York: Doral Publishing, 1990.

Davis, Kathy Diamond. *Therapy Dogs*. New York: Howell Book House, 1992.

Gallup, Davis Anne. *Running With Man's Best Friend*. Loveland, Colo.: Alpine Publications, 1986.

Habgood, Dawn and Robert. *On the Road Again With Man's Best Friend*. New England, Mid-Atlantic, West Coast and Southeast editions. Selective guides to area bed and breakfasts, inns, hotels and resorts that welcome guests and their dogs. New York: Howell Book House, 1995.

Holland, Vergil S. *Herding Dogs*. New York: Howell Book House, 1994.

LaBelle, Charlene G. *Backpacking With Your Dog*. Loveland, Colo.: Alpine Publications, 1993.

Simmons-Moake, Jane. *Agility Training, The Fun Sport for All Dogs*. New York: Howell Book House, 1991.

Spencer, James B. *Hup! Training Flushing Spaniels the American Way*. New York: Howell Book House, 1992.

Spencer, James B. *Point! Training the All-Seasons Birddog*. New York: Howell Book House, 1995.

Tarrant, Bill. *Training the Hunting Retriever*. New York: Howell Book House, 1991.

Volhard, Jack and Wendy. *The Canine Good Citizen*. New York: Howell Book House, 1994.

General Titles

Haggerty, Captain Arthur J. *How to Get Your Pet Into Show Business*. New York: Howell Book House, 1994.

McLennan, Bardi. *Dogs and Kids, Parenting Tips*. New York: Howell Book House, 1993.

Moran, Patti J. *Pet Sitting for Profit, A Complete Manual for Professional Success*. New York: Howell Book House, 1992.

Scalisi, Danny and Libby Moses. *When Rover Just Won't Do, Over 2,000 Suggestions for Naming Your Dog.* New York: Howell Book House, 1993.

Sife, Wallace, PhD. *The Loss of a Pet.* New York: Howell Book House, 1993.

Wrede, Barbara J. *Civilizing Your Puppy.* Hauppauge, N.Y.: Barron's Educational Series, 1992.

Magazines

The AKC GAZETTE, The Official Journal for the Sport of Purebred Dogs. American Kennel Club, 51 Madison Ave., New York, NY.

Bloodlines Journal. United Kennel Club, 100 E. Kilgore Rd., Kalamazoo, MI.

Dog Fancy. Fancy Publications, 3 Burroughs, Irvine, CA 92718

Dog World. Maclean Hunter Publishing Corp., 29 N. Wacker Dr., Chicago, IL 60606.

Videos

"SIRIUS Puppy Training," by Ian Dunbar, PhD, MRCVS. James & Kenneth Publishers, 2140 Shattuck Ave. #2406, Berkeley, CA 94704. Order from the publisher.

"Training the Companion Dog," from Dr. Dunbar's British TV Series, James & Kenneth Publishers. (See address above).

The American Kennel Club produces videos on every breed of dog, as well as on hunting tests, field trials and other areas of interest to purebred dog owners. For more information, write to AKC/Video Fulfillment, 5580 Centerview Dr., Suite 200, Raleigh, NC 27606.

chapter 13

Resources

Breed Clubs

Every breed recognized by the American Kennel Club has a national (parent) club. National clubs are a great source of information on your breed. You can get the name of the secretary of the club by contacting:

The American Kennel Club
51 Madison Avenue
New York, NY 10010
(212) 696-8200

There are also numerous all-breed, individual breed, obedience, hunting and other special-interest dog clubs across the country. The American Kennel Club can provide you with a geographical list of clubs to find ones in your area. Contact them at the above address.

Registry Organizations

Registry organizations register purebred dogs. The American Kennel Club is the oldest and largest in this country, and currently recognizes over 130 breeds. The United Kennel Club registers some breeds the AKC doesn't (including the American Pit Bull Terrier and the Miniature Fox Terrier) as well as many of the same breeds. The others included here are for your reference; the AKC can provide you with a list of foreign registries.

American Kennel Club
51 Madison Avenue
New York, NY 10010

United Kennel Club (UKC)
100 E. Kilgore Road
Kalamazoo, MI 49001-5598

American Dog Breeders Assn.
P.O. Box 1771
Salt Lake City, UT 84110
(Registers American Pit Bull Terriers)

Canadian Kennel Club
89 Skyway Avenue
Etobicoke, Ontario
Canada M9W 6R4

National Stock Dog Registry
P.O. Box 402
Butler, IN 46721
(Registers working stock dogs)

Orthopedic Foundation for Animals (OFA)
2300 E. Nifong Blvd.
Columbia, MO 65201-3856
(Hip registry)

Activity Clubs

Write to these organizations for information on the
activities they sponsor.

American Kennel Club
51 Madison Avenue
New York, NY 10010
(Conformation Shows, Obedience Trials, Field
Trials and Hunting Tests, Agility, Canine Good

Citizen, Lure Coursing, Herding, Tracking, Earthdog Tests, Coonhunting.)

United Kennel Club
100 E. Kilgore Road
Kalamazoo, MI 49001-5598
(Conformation Shows, Obedience Trials, Agility, Hunting for Various Breeds, Terrier Trials and more.)

North American Flyball Assn.
1342 Jeff St.
Ypsilanti, MI 48198

International Sled Dog Racing Assn.
P.O. Box 446
Norman, ID 83848-0446

North American Working Dog Assn., Inc.
Southeast Kreisgruppe
P.O. Box 833
Brunswick, GA 31521

Trainers

Association of Pet Dog Trainers
P.O. Box 3734
Salinas, CA 93912
(408) 663–9257

American Dog Trainers' Network
161 West 4th St.
New York, NY 10014
(212) 727–7257

National Association of Dog Obedience Instructors
2286 East Steel Rd.
St. Johns, MI 48879

Associations

American Dog Owners Assn.
1654 Columbia Tpk.
Castleton, NY 12033
(Combats anti-dog legislation)

Delta Society
P.O. Box 1080
Renton, WA 98057-1080
(Promotes the human/animal bond through
pet-assisted therapy and other programs)

Dog Writers Assn. of America (DWAA)
Sally Cooper, Secy.
222 Woodchuck Ln.
Harwinton, CT 06791

National Assn. for Search and Rescue (NASAR)
P.O. Box 3709
Fairfax, VA 22038

Therapy Dogs International
1536 Morris Place
Hillside, NJ 07205